WHAT EVERYONE SHOULD KNOW ABOUT

ISLAM AND MUSLIMS

By
Suzanne Haneef

Islamic Book Service

© Islamic Book Service

What Everyone Should Know About
Islam and Muslim

ISBN: 81-7231-322-5

Reprint Edition - 2006

Published by *Abdul Naeem* for
Islamic Book Service
2872, Kucha Chelan, Darya Ganj,
New Delhi-110 002 (INDIA)
Ph.: 011- 23244556,23247899, 23253514,
        23286551, 55360867,(Direct)
        Fax: 23277913
islamic@eth.net
E-mail: ibsdelhi@del2.vsnl.net.in
Website: www.islamic-india.com

Printed at: Globe Offset Press ,Darya Ganj,New Delhi-110002

CONTENTS

Title	*Page No.*

Bismillahir-Rahmanir-Raheem
In the name of Allah the Merciful, the Mercy-Giving

A WORD TO THE READER

Perhaps you have been hearing a lot about Islam and Muslims in the news and are interested in knowing, justifiably, just what this religion is all about. Or, perhaps, you know some Muslims and have been stirred to curiosity about the faith they profess. Or, perhaps, someone you know, may be even someone in your own family, has decided to embrace Islam. If so, this book is meant for you. Its purpose is to set forth the Islamic concepts and beliefs in a clear, understandable manner and then to give you an idea about how Muslims are supposed to live. In short, it presents a summary of the Islamic beliefs, ways of worship, qualities, values, morals, standards of conduct, and, in concrete and practical terms, the Islamic way of life.

I think you will agree with me that a religion which does not demand anything of its followers, or which leaves those who have newly entered into it more or less where they were before they embraced it, is an ineffective religion, a mere set of "beliefs" or rituals which does not affect the conduct of living. Islam does not fit this description. For Islam is not a mere belief-system, an ideology or a religion in the usual sense in which these words are understood. Rather it is a total way of life, a complete system governing all aspects of man's existence, both individual and collective. It is in fact a religion which, as I hope to demonstrate in the course of this book, frees the human being from domination by his material and animal aspects and makes him truly *human*.

The meaning of the word *Islam* is "submission" and "peace." In the course of making an individual *Muslim*—that is, one who is

in a state of *Islam* or submission to the One True God—Islam
profoundly affects his thinking and behaviour. Indeed, there is no
aspect of a person's life, nor of the life of the society which is
made up of such people, which it does not touch and transform in
keeping with its basic concept, that of the Lordship and Sovereignty
of God and man's responsibility to Him. Islam's first requirement
is belief and its second, action. Out of its concepts and beliefs, a
certain attitude toward life, toward one's own self, toward other
human beings, toward the universe; a certain kind of personality;
a distinctive type of human interaction; a particular mode of
worship, of family life, manners, living habits and so on in relation
to all aspects of life, takes its development.

We live in an age of tremendous upheaval and uncertainty.
People everywhere are groping anxiously for something that can
save humanity, which has lost its way and is on the brink of
unprecedented disaster. It may be true that today we live in an era
of the ultimate in material civilization and progress, but in the
realm of values and morals mankind appears to be close to
bankruptcy. In the Islamic view, these problems are fundamentally
of a spiritual nature, the result of man's having lost sight of who
he is in relation to himself, to other human beings, and above all
to God, in Whom being itself, and all human relationships, originate.
And until he is able to find meaningful and correct answers to the
ultimate questions, and solutions to his problems which are compatible
with the fundamental realities of existence and his own nature, his
life will remain adrift without a base and without a direction, his
personality will be distorted and fragmented, his human nature
abused by permitting its animal part to dominate, and his societies
full of overwhelming problems.

Islamic claims to provide such answers and solutions, ones
which are compatible with reason, logic, the realities of the
physical universe, and with human nature itself. For Islam is,
above all, a view of the total Reality, encompassing the existence
and attributes of the Creator, man's relationship with Him, his role
and purpose in this world, and the relationship between this life
and the life of the Hereafter, which puts all that exists into proper
perspective and gives balance and direction to the life of human
beings and their societies.

However, Islam is so little known and understood in the Western world that to many people, especially in America, it is simply another strange religious cult or sect, Allah is some sort of a heathen diety, Muhammad is someone who is worshipped by hordes of pagans overseas, and Muslims are either militant sword-wielding bedouins mounted on camels, fanatical men of religion with long robes and beards, or rich, decadent playboys. Indeed, Islam has been so gravely misunderstood and misrepresented in the West that many people in America and Europe think of it as an enemy to any sort of stability, peace and progress; they mistrust it, fear it and regard it as a dire threat without as a rule knowing anything about it other than what the popular media convey, which almost invariably reflects grave inaccuracies and errors. As these lines are written, the media are full of such "news" and views about Islam and Muslims; daily one can hear or read item after item on the subject. Virtually without exception these mis-represent not only the details of the Islamic system and the motivations and characters of sincere Muslims, but also the fundamental concepts and teachings of the religion. They are often so gravely distorted that, indeed, a Muslim who encounters them may not even be able to recognize that they are concerned with the religion he has known and practiced all his life. The Western world today is full of "experts" on Islam who consider themselves far more knowledgeable about it than the Muslims who are living it day by day, but who seldom if ever take the trouble to understand Islam, especially its central world-view and basic concepts, on a deeper level.

Why is all this so? First, it is due in part to the legacy of history. Islam and Christendom confronted each other as enemies during the Crusades and afterwards, and the propaganda against the enemy and its beliefs and way of life which is common during times of conflict, whether it is true or false, has never yet been laid to rest in the Western world. Second, it is partly due to the confused and distorted picture of Islam which the behaviour of many Muslims, those who profess this faith but do not live by it, often doing everything which it does not permit and doing nothing which it requires, very unfortunately presents. It is also due in part to the fact that many people in the Western world think of any religious system in terms of Christian concepts and values, or in terms of the concepts of Western civilization, which do not necessarily fit with or apply to Islam. And finally, it is also undoubtedly due to the fact that many people in the West, particularly in America, have such an unquestioning conviction of the innate superiority and rightness of the American or Western way of life that they do not consider it necessary or important to be accurately informed about others' viewpoints and ways of life. To many of us Muslims remain, undifferentiatedly, "those people over there," whose only possible utility or interest is in relation to whether or not they will sell us the oil we need or boost our economy by buying our goods. We often regard them, with secret satisfaction in our own superiority as the advanced people of the West, as simple, child like beings whose world-view must *ipso facto* be wrong because ours is right.

All too few people in the Western world realize that the followers of Islam constitute the second largest religious community in the world today (the first being Christianity). It is the faith professed by nearly eight hundred million people living in every part of the globe, including the countries of the West, with the largest numbers concentrated in the region between North Africa and Malaysia. Hence, if for no reason other than its tremendous relevance to the contemporary world, Islam and its followers surely deserve to be represented accurately and understood correctly by anyone who desires to be well-informed and aware. In addition, since today there are large numbers of people who profess Islam, both foreign-born Muslims and Western converts, living in America and in Europe where Islam is the second largest religious community at the present time, Islam also deserves to be known and understood correctly as a faith which increasingly has more and more relevance to the religious community of the Western world.

I would like, therefore, to request the reader, for the sake of fairness and objectivity as he approaches this brief study of Islam, to try his best to clear his mind of any preconceptions he may have about Islam, whether these have been gathered from the news, movies or television programmes, from newspaper or magazine articles, or simply the vague, piece-meal picture of Islam and

Muslims which one somehow picks up from here and there, or any combination of these. As a rule such presentations do not constitute reliable or authoritative sources of information about either Islam or Muslims and are, in fact, often the propagators of misconceptions, fallacies and prejudices rather than of accurate information. If, therefore, the reader can set aside temporarily whatever he may have gleaned from such sources concerning the subject, hopefully when he has finished reading this book (and, if he is interested, others from among the titles listed at the end of this volume) he will be in a much better position to determine what part is accurate and what part is false and misleading.

In writing this book, I have been all too keenly aware that to present Islam as it should be presented is at once a great challenge and an almost overwhelming responsibility. I have undertaken this responsibility with a great sense of inadequacy for the task, for there are countless other Muslims who are far better qualified for it both in terms of their knowledge and their practice of Islam. Nonetheless, to do so has been felt as a duty. Many books about Islam are available, but virtually all of them are either by non-Muslim authors who invariably reflect many blatant distortions and prejudices against Islam or by Muslims whose writings, although they may portray Islam correctly and indeed often with great depth and meaningfulness, are not really geared to a non-Muslim Western readership. Since I have myself, in the process of coming to an understanding of Islam, gone through the simultaneous process of asking and finding answers to the questions which have been asked, and hopefully answered, in this volume, I have felt an obligation to share this understanding with others who may be interested in knowing what Islam is or what it can offer to mankind. It is my earnest prayer that God will accept this small effort and make it useful for a better understanding of Islam, the path of peace and submission to Him.

Suzanne Haneef

SECTION ONE:

Beliefs and Worships

BELIEFS

I. The Islamic creed

"La ilaha illa Allah, Muhammadu Rasool Allah"— "There is no diety except Allah, Muhammad is the Messenger of Allah." This simple statement of a Muslim's basic beliefs is the starting point for all that follows. From this expression of belief in the Oneness and Uniqueness of Allah and the messengership of Muhammad stem all of Islam's concepts, attitudes, moral values and guidelines for human behaviour and relationships.

How can all this follow from this one simple and seemingly quite obvious statement?

Thus: The first part of this declaration, *"La ilaha illa Allah."* attests not only to the Oneness and Uniqueness of Allah, *the* Deity, it signifies, at the same time, the oneness of the lordship, the sovereignty and the authority in he universe and this world. For when we affirm that there is no deity except the One Allah, we are actually stating that, as there is no other Creator and Sustainer of the universe, this world and all that is in them, there can likewise be no other Ruler, Law-Giver and Supreme Authority for mankind. Allah, the Lord of all creation, creates what He pleases, giving each of His creations the nature, function and role which He desires for it; in this He is accountable to no one and all things are under His absolute control. The purpose for which He created human beings is to acknowledge, worship and obey Him alone, and at the same time to manage the affairs of this world and administer it with justice and righteousness according to His all-wise laws.

How do we know all this? How can a mere human being, a very limited and finite creature, know about Allah—that is, about Infinity—and His purposes for mankind, the answers to the multitude of Basic questions which encompass Allah's nature and attributes, man's relationship to Him, and why he has been put into this world? We are living in an era in which we have increasingly lost the conviction of the meaning and purpose of existence; indeed, the entire complex of modern civilization seems to proclaim the utter purposelessness and meaninglessness of life. Then how *can* we know?

Indeed, these are the most vital and Basic questions for any human being. Without satisfactory answers to them, life makes no sense, it has neither purpose nor meaning, and one is simply going through the motions of living without any reason other than the fact that he happens to be alive. Hence the essential task facing each individual is to search for the answers to these questions until he finds them and, when he has found them, to acknowledge their truth and to live by them as faithfully as he can. But the question remains: Where are the answers to them to be found?

Assuredly, if (as many people believe) religion were simply a device invented by man to explain the world of nature or for ordering human affairs, human beings would have been able to arrive at satisfactory answers to these questions through their own reasoning and observation and to guide their lives by them in a suitable manner; the worship of the forces of nature, spirits and demons, sticks and stones and gods made by human hands and mythological figures connected to the world of men by their semi-human nature represents various efforts on their part to do so throughout the course of history. But to arrive at the objective *truth:* at a correct knowledge of the meaning and purpose of existence, the nature and attributes of the Creator of all things, and of men's role and ultimate destiny, by man's unaided efforts is an obvious impossibility since it concerns what is totally outside the realm of human observation or deductive faculties; even if some individuals should, by their own efforts, succeed at grasping some part of these truths, they would have no certain or positive means of verifying them.

For the only possible means by which human beings can have access to an unquestionably correct understanding of such matters is if the Source of everything, the willing, acting, sustaining Power

Whom we call Allah, Himself imparts this knowledge to us by whatever means He may deem fit. And this is precisely the significance of the second part of Islam's Declaration of faith, "..... *Muhammadu Rasool Allah*" — Muhammad is the Messenger of Allah.

Since the dawn of true human consciousness, Islam asserts, the Creator not only implanted in human beings the awareness of His existence, the innate knowledge that there is non-corporeal, transcendent Being Who created them and the world around them:[1] He also provided them with the answers to these vital questions which have occupied their minds since their emergence as thinking, questioning, problem-solving beings on this planet, conveying His guidance to humankind through various individuals whom He chose as His message-bearers to different groups of people: to be the connecting link between Himself and man, so to speak. Through the passing of time and changes occasioned by human error, much of the Message which they brought was lost. However, enough remains of the earlier scriptures or the teachings of earlier messengers—of the revelations entrusted by Allah to such prophets as Abraham, Moses, Jesus and many others (Allah's peace and blessings be on them all) — to make it very clear that this Message has been basically one and the same throughout history: that there is a single, unique Being Who is the Lord and Master of all creation; that this Being has made laws to govern the conduct of human beings; and that each individual is accountable to this Being for how he lives his life.

Thus Islam does not claim to be a new religion. Rather it is the *original* religion, that primordial faith which has had its roots deep in man's consciousness since the first true human being walked upon earth *because the Creator Himself implanted it there*, the faith revealed to and preached by all the prophets: the religion of

---

1. Even when, during the course of history, human beings have wandered away from belief in Allah as the sole Sustainer and Controller of all that exists, they have not as a rule denied the fact of His *existence*. Rather they have invented associates or partners in His divinity, ascribing some part of His powers to them while simultaneously acknowledging His supremacy over them.

submission and accountability to the One Allah. Islam teaches the Divine origin of this message, pointing to the similarity and continuity of the teachings brought by the various messengers of Allah throughout history, but it makes it clear that in the course of time they were changed and grave distortions appeared among them. Hence the Divine origin of these messages is to be believed in but not necessarily their present form or content, since their present condition makes it impossible to determine what part of them has been changed, either accidentally or deliberately, by the hands of men.

Each one of the prophets was a man like other men, with the same human needs and feelings; Islam most emphatically denies any suggestion of the divinity or super-human nature of Allah's messengers. At the same time, they were men of special qualities whom Allah singled out from the rest of humanity for the task of conveying His guidance. The prophets are characterized by their total submission to Allah and their nearness to Him, their pure and upright natures, the extraordinary righteousness of their conduct, and their unswerving commitment to the mission with which they were entrusted.

The guidance revealed suited the mentality and needs of the particular peoples to whom it was addressed. Consequently, many earlier prophets were sent with miracles and signs since the people of their eras, whose belief in Allah was very weak or altogether lacking, were willing to acknowledge Him only when His existence and power were demonstrated by such proofs. At length, when the mind of man had developed to its full potential, Allah raised His last prophet, Muhammad, an Arab descended from Abraham, with the final and complete statement of His guidance for all time to come. And it is because Muslims follow the guidance which was conveyed through Muhammad (may Allah's peace and blessings be on him), the guidance which carries the complete and final proclamation of Allah's laws and commands for humankind, that *"Muhammadu Rasool Allah"* — Muhammad is the Messenger of Allah — is so significant and vital as to form the second part of the Muslim's statement of faith.

Far from being a state of degradation and servility, the human individual's exclusive submission to the Creator alone invests him with greatness and sublimity, for by means of it he is freed from obeying and serving anything less than Allah, the only Being Who can ever be worthy of his devotion and obedience. *"La ilaha illa Allah, Muhammadu Rasool Allah"* is therefore that powerful statement of faith which represents the liberations of the one who profess it from servitude and submission to anything or anyone other than Allah Most High. It is the denial of all other claimants to divinity and supreme authority, the affirmation of Allah's Oneness and Sovereignty, and the statement of belief in and acceptance of His guidance as revealed to Prophet Muhammad (peace be on him), the last of Allah's messengers.

II. The Islamic View of Reality

Every human being who comes into the world must deal, at one level or another, with the question of what constitutes Reality. Consciously or otherwise, each one of us lives with his own individual understanding of what makes up the totality of existence. This reality concept determines to a great extent how we relate to the universe, our comprehension of the purpose of our existence, and what role we play in this world.

Is the physical universe—what we can see, touch, measure or perceive with our faculties or instruments—all there is, or is there something more? Where did we come from, and where do we go from here? Is it all the result of blind chance and randomness, or is it part of a purposeful, meaningful scheme and plan? Is there Someone in charge of it all Who is Himself the Ultimate Reality, or not? Does man's life itself have any reason or ultimate significance, or is man just a perishable physical entity who will cease to exist like all other living things? Is this life the only life, or will it be followed by some other state of existence, and if so, of what kind?

In fact, an individual's conception of Reality—his answers to these and many other related questions—is nothing less than his basic orientation to the universe, his perception of his place and the role he is to play in it. Upon this conception rests, in effect, all that a human being is and strives to become, his relationship with himself, with others and with the world around him, and above all, with his Creator.

.At this time in history many people are asking, "Is there really Anyone out there or not? And if there is, does it really matter?" Such questions are a mirror of modern man's total alienation from himself and from his Source, and, as a result, from the universe and his fellow human beings as well. The technology-oriented, mechanized environment of the Western world has trained many people to disbelieve in what is termed "the supernatural," even though they may profess to believe in Allah. Science, one of the greatest of present-day man's deities, has taught us to regard as having reality only that which can be seen, observed, measured or perceived through man's senses, mental capacities or inventions. Consequently, while many people in the Western world today may not absolutely deny the existence of what they are unable to perceive, in practice they often act as if it does not exist by ignoring it altogether, or feeling that even if it does exist it has no relevance or importance in the scheme of things. Although many people profess to "believe" in Allah, this is often a static belief, a mere opinion that Allah exists rather than that He does not exist which has no significant practical consequence and does not in any way affect the way they live their lives.

Others do believe, and very strongly, in "the supernatural." However, their beliefs are incomplete and unreliable, depending largely on guesswork. The accuracy and validity of such beliefs cannot in any way be depended upon since they are based on one's own or others' subjective experiences; hence they cannot be taken seriously as a means of gaining accurate knowledge of the ultimate Reality of existence, especially of Allah as the Centre and Source of the Reality, nor as constituting valid guidance for the living of man's life. The current preoccupation with extrasensory phenomena may be a step in the direction of acceptance of a Reality greater than the physical universe, but it consists largely of speculation coupled with the attempt to subject nonmaterial phenomena to scientific analysis which must, in the long run due to the nature of the material under study, be self-defeating; moreover it cannot by any means address itself to the question of Allah's nature or attributes, or even His existence. That many psychic phenomena created to and inspired by Satan rather than being spiritual experiences connected to Allah seems a strong probability, and hence such phenomena are a very uncertain and risky foundation for either beliefs or for living.

Islam deals in a clear, straightforward manner with all these issues. In fact, Islam itself poses the questions asked above and many more, insisting that meaningful answers to them, compatible with the observed phenomena of the universe and with reason, must be sought by anyone who possesses a mind.

There is a realm of existence, Islam proclaims, which is not accessible to human sense or awareness nor bound by the limitations of the human intellect. This realm which is beyond man's perception is termed *al-Ghaib*, that is, the Hidden or Unseen, while that which is known and perceptible is termed *ash-Shahdah*, the Evident or Witnessed. And in Islam belief in this unseen realm is a prerequisite for belief in and understanding of and of that part of His creation which man's senses and faculties cannot perceive but which is nonetheless of fundamental importance to his existence. The section which follows, concerning Islam's Articles of Faith, deals with these Unseen Realities.

Islam asserts that what is visible and perceptible to human faculties—*ash-Shahadah*—is only a part, and perhaps a very small and insignificant part, of the totality of what exists. Although man cannot grasp the totality of existence, this does not in any way negate the reality of more than he is able to grasp any more than, say, an ant or an elephant can determine the totality of what exists on the basis of its limited experience and perceptions. The fact, which it is often strangely painful for many of us to admit, is simply that man is a quite finite, limited being with faculties and understanding which are equipped to take in and comprehend just so much and no more. Yet the "more" is there nevertheless, that wider Reality, the totality of which is known only to its Creator.

For the existence of this wider Reality, although it cannot be perceived directly, there are many evidences which are known to us all. Among these is the physical universe itself, which speaks in endless volumes about the unimaginable power, wisdom and creativity of Allah. The human being is another striking evidence. He comes from somewhere, from non-being into being, and when he dies it is obvious that the most vital part of him is gone. In his spiritual feelings and aspirations, too, man's longing for something deeper and higher than the material sphere, there are clear intimations of the existence of a non-material realm of the greatest importance, to which the human being is in some unknown way so intimately bound up that to ignore or reject it must inevitably result in very serious consequences to the individual and his society. Religious feelings, expressions and movements are common to all human beings, and many of them possess similar features and characteriztics. In particular, the great monotheistic religions—Judaism, Christianity and Islam—demonstrate very striking similarities, pointing unmistakably to their common origin in the same Source, Allah Most High. And finally, various extrasensory phenomena, among which we may include dreams and premonitions relating to future events and many other striking manifestations of the existence of a non-material realm, provide us with some dramatic clues concerning the Unseen Reality.

In Islam Allah is the centre of that Reality; indeed, He is *the* Reality. Allah is the One Who does everything, the Creator and Sustainer of all that exists, the Provider of all things with their sustenance. He is the Alternator of night and day, the One Who creates what He wills in the wombs of the mothers, Who renews the earth after it is dead and brings out of it, by means of rain from the sky and nourishment within the ground, the growing things which constitute food for men and beasts. And it is He Who gives a term of life to His creatures as He sees fit. It is He Who will bring forth the bodies of men from their graves and join them to their souls on that awesome Day — concerning which there is no doubt—when He will bring the universe to an end, and it is He Who will judge them according to the most absolute and impartial standards of justice and mercy. He is the Supreme, the Irresistible, the All-Knowing and the All-Wise, the One Who is accountable to no one but to Whom all things are accountable, Who does what He wills with His creation, and before Whom all things bow in submission, and at the same time He is also the Merciful, the Gracious, the Loving and the Forgiving.

This is Islam's view of Reality, the view of Reality held by countless Muslims throughout the world. Such concepts form a vital part of the Muslim's consciousness, beginning in early childhood. He grows up with the awareness of Allah's reality and power, His beneficence and kindness to His creations; with the realization that this life is only a very small part of a Reality so vast that the mind of a human being cannot conceive of it except in an extremely limited manner; and with the knowledge that it is not the final stage of his existence, which is a continuous one. As there was a time when, in the words of the Qur'an, man was "a thing not (even) mention able" (76:1), so Allah brought him out of non-being into existence: from a sperm and an egg in the bodies of his parents into an embryo growing in his mother's womb, then into independent life when he was born into the world; from helpless infancy into childhood, and from maturity into old age during which he becomes like a weak, helpless child all over again; and from thence into another Life which will be the final state of all human beings. In that Life, those who acknowledged Allah as their Lord, followed His guidance and strove to please Him will be in a condition of enduring happiness and felicity beyond the capacity of the human mind to imagine, while those who denied Him and devoted themselves to deities other than Allah, rejecting His guidance and living for themselves or for their lusts and passions, will be in an unimaginably fearful state of agony and torment in keeping with the state of their own souls.

Islam also proclaims that human nature has its own reality. While various Western philosophies or theories concerning man conceive of him as a glorified machine, a being who reacts mechanically as "programmed" by his emotions, environment or biochemical processes, or, conversely, as a higher kind of animal, the Islamic conception is very different, and such materialistic approaches are seen as extremely false, misleading representations of the true nature of man. For man, Islam asserts, is a unique creation of Allah's possessing an obvious, outwards aspect—the physical body—and a hidden, inner aspect—the mind, emotions and soul. The uniqueness of man's nature lies in the fact that he has been endowed with freedom of choice and judgment between right and wrong, capacities for thinking, transmitting knowledge, feeling and acting which have not been given to other creatures, and an immortal soul which lives on after the death of the physical body. Thus man is a composite of many aspects, levels and functions, the totality of which represents the reality of human nature.

Allah has created man with this complex and multi-faceted nature, Islam asserts, not so that there may be war and strife between the various elements but in order that they may form a smoothly-functioning, harmonious whole. This in itself constitutes the great task, the ultimate challenge, of being human. Each element of man's nature has its role and function, its legitimate needs and right to satisfaction; but in order to bring about the harmony which Allah intends, among them, the individual must exercise the power of his will and govern them according to the laws which Allah has laid down for his well-being, thus achieving synthesis, integration and balance within his personality. This is why Islam concerns itself not merely with "religious" and "spiritual" matters but with all aspects of human life, all of which fall within the framework of religion in the Islamic sense of the term, treating man as an indivisible, organic whole in keeping with the reality of his uniquely human nature.

Such a correct understanding of man's true nature and his place in the scheme of things is of vital importance in the Islamic framework. By means of Allah's guidance conveyed through the prophets, man has been shown how the reality of his nature fits into the total Reality and has been informed what is expected of him in relation to that Reality, the centre and focus of which is Allah Most High. In this way he will be able to live in harmony and balance rather than in conflict and chaos during his brief journey from one phase of this Reality—this earthly life—to the next, that is, the enduring life of the Hereafter, thereby achieving true worth and true success both in this world and in the World-to-Come.

III. The Articles of Faith[1]

1. Allah (Allah)

"Say (O Muhammad): 'He is Allah, the One, the Self-

---

1 The Articles of Faith, although numbered in this presentation, are not in any fixed sequential order, for they are independent and simultaneous principles. Hence they may appear in different orders in various presentations of Islam.

Sufficient. He begets not nor is He begotten, and there is none like Him.'"   (The Holy Qur'an 112:1-4)

"Whatever is in the heavens and on earth glorifies Allah, for He is the Mighty, the Wise. To Him belongs the dominion of the heavens and the earth. It is He Who gives life and death, and He has power over all things. He is the First and the Last, the Evident and the Immanent, and He has full knowledge of all things. It is He Who created the heavens and the earth in six days (stages or eons), and is moreover firmly established on the throne (of authority). He knows what enters into the earth and what comes forth from it, and what descends from the heavens and what mounts up to it; and He is with you wherever you may be. And Allah sees all that you do. To Him belongs the dominion of the heavens and the earth, and all affairs are referred back to Allah, He merges night into day and He merges day into night. And He has full knowledge of what is in the breasts (of men)."   (57:1-6)

Let us now look further at the Islamic conception of Allah, the first of Islam's fundamental Articles of Faith. To what extent does it resemble the conceptions of Allah taught by other religions and in what way is it unique and different?

In nearly all religions, the conception of Allah is to a greater or lesser extent bound up with the limitations of His creatures; one could cite innumerable examples from various creeds attesting to this. However, Islam emphatically proclaims that Allah the Most High and Exalted, the Creator and Sustainer of all that exists, is far above possessing any of the creaturely attributes which have been ascribed to Him, nor is He bound by any of the limitations of human beings or of anything else He has created. He has no body nor form, no physical attributes or characteriztics. Rather His attributes are those of One Who is above any sort of limitations, such as having a beginning or an end, begetting or being begotten, or physical dimensions or needs such as requiring food, rest or procreating; for He is the One Who gives such dimensions and attributes to His creatures, while He Himself does not share them in the slightest degree. The Qur'an says:

"Allah is He other than Whom there is no deity. He

knows the Unseen (*al-Ghaib*) and the Evident (*ash-Shahdah*). He is the Merciful, the Mercy-Giving, Allah is He than Whom there is no deity—the Sovereign, the Holy One, the Source of Peace, the Guardian of Faith, the Preserver of Safety, the Mighty, the Irresistible, the Supreme. Glory be to Allah! (high is He) above the partners they attributes to Him. He is Allah, the Creator, the Evolver, the Bestower of Forms. To Him belong the most beautiful names. Whatever is in the heavens and on earth glorifies Him, and He is the Mighty, the Wise." (59:22-24)

One who ponders over the nature of Allah with an open mind in relation to the observed facts of the universe has no choice but to realize that He cannot, by definition, be simply a sort of superman Who sits above the clouds and directs affairs, while sharing in creaturely needs and attributes. For Allah is nothing less than the Originator and Fashioner of the universe with all its vast and perfect systems, the One Who sustains and keeps it functioning according to His infinitely wise plans and laws. And thus it is clear and certain—as Islam emphatically proclaims—that He is infinitely beyond anything which the mind or senses of man can grasp or comprehend or imagine or explain, and that He is far, far above having any similarity to any of His creation. For He alone is the Creator and everything else is the created; He alone is Divine, and no human being or any other creature can ever share His divinity or His unique attributes as Creator and Sustainer in the slightest degree. In short, Allah Most High has not the least resemblance to the limited, petty gods with their semi-human nature which the minds of men, due to their imperfect knowledge and understanding, have invented to supply the deficiencies in their comprehension but who, at the same time, fall so short of being Allah-like. His Divine nature is entirely unique and can be grasped only through the contemplation of His attributes and His creation. The Qur'an says:

"Allah! There is no deity except Him, the Living, the Eternal. No slumber can overpower Him nor sleep. His are all things in the heavens and on earth. Who is there who can intercede in His presence except as He permits? He knows what is before them and what is hidden from them, and they cannot comprehend anything of His

> knowledge except what He wills. His kingdom spreads
> over the heavens and the earth, and the guarding of them
> does not weary Him, and He is the Exalted, the Almighty."
>
> (2:255)

Yet Allah's existence does not have the least relevance for mankind if He is not actively concerned with His creation, or if (as some people imagine) He created the universe and men and then went off and forgot about them, leaving them on their own to sink or swim. But Islam proclaims that Allah is *the* Reality, and thus His existence has absolute relevance and meaning for every single human being *since it is solely in relation to Allah that we exist and move through the journey of this life on our way back to Him.* Islam, then, asserts that Allah is always active and is concerned and creatively involved with every single part of His creation, from the vastest of stars down to the very atoms which comprise them, with every part of its macro-and micro-systems, and that it exists, continues and fulfills its functions by His command and will. For His concern is not merely in creating but also in sustaining, directing and guiding: in providing for His creations, maintaining, ordering and regulating them, and, in respect to human beings, in giving them the direction necessary for living their lives in this world in such a manner as will ensure their everlasting good in the Life-to-Come.

Allah is not concerned with man, however, as the sole or necessarily the most important of His creations, but as the one creature on earth (which is only one part of His unimaginably vast and complex creation) whom He has endowed with a thinking mind, a feeling heart, the ability to store and transmit knowledge, and to whom He has given freedom of choice. At the same time, Allah asks man to use this freedom of choice to voluntarily and deliberately choose what Allah wants for him rather than to follow his own random and often chaotic desires; that is, to submit his will to Allah's higher will and by this means to carry out the responsibilities, both personal and collective, which Allah has entrusted to him. For not only does the Creator have the absolute right to make whatever rules or laws He sees fit for His creatures, but He also has the absolute right to their obedience. At the same time, He alone possesses the all-embracing, absolute knowledge

and wisdom to provide His creatures with such guidance as will
lead to their assured well-being both in this world and in the
Hereafter.

Such a belief in Allah and man's relationship to Him, however,
is for the conscientious Muslim no mere intellectual exercise. For
as he believes that Allah alone is the Master of the universe, the
Lord of men, the sole Authority and Legislator; and that man is
nothing but a humble slave before Him, it follows that there must
be no other lords and authorities in his life besides Allah. Islam
proclaims that all other elements which claim man's obedience and
devotion, and which attempt to rule or dominate his life, are false
and are in competition with Allah for lordship over him. It insists
that one who truly and wholeheartedly believes that Allah alone is
the sole and rightful Sovereign and Law-Giver must not and will
not obey or give his devotion or allegience to other claimants to
authority and sovereignty. Rather he must reject them all, submit
himself to Allah alone, and strive with all his energies against the
domination of deities other than Allah.

A little thought will make it clear that no matter how free an
individual may consider himself to be, nevertheless he submits to
some authority, his life is oriented around some goal, and his
loyalty and devotion are given to someone or something. Every
single one of us submits to and worships some deity which holds
sway over our hearts, and either this deity is Allah Himself or it
is, in every case without exception something lesser than Allah
since *everything* is lesser than He. Such a deity may be a human
being such as a ruler, religious figure, philosopher or a member of
one's family; it may be some man-made ideology, philosophy
or-ism. Such worship may be taking "productivity," "progress,"
"work," or "the state" as one's idol; it may be love of self, pride
in family, descent, race, Education, occupation, wealth, status or
intelligence; it may be catering to one's own desires and becoming
enslaved by them. Or it may be deifying science or the arts, or
becoming the slave of fads and fashions, pleasures and lusts and
passions, personal habits or the demands of society, or any of the
thousand-and-one deities of man's own invention which are known
to all of us, which effectually replace the lordship of Allah Most
High over our hearts and lives.

We have spoken of man's attributes of freedom of choice. But this does not apply simply to the various single decisions which one makes every day of his life in matters big and small. Such choices depend, in fact, upon the basic, central choice which one makes to direct the whole of his existence. The greatest and most fundamental choice which every human being is called upon to make is to decide who is his Lord, for whom he lives his life, to whom is his goal, and who he worships, serves and obeys. Indeed, Islam emphatically proclaims, the choice is between only two possible ways:

to be in bondage to human ideas and notions and desires, or to consciously and voluntarily commit oneself to be bound by the standards, criteria and laws of Allah alone;

to be the slave of human masters, living by man-made values, philosophies and doctrines, or to be the slave of the true Master of men, Allah the Praised and Exalted;

to be satisfied to live and work for something lesser, or to dedicate oneself to living and striving for the only One Who can be worthy of such devotion from a human being, the only One Who can truly guide and give meaning to man's life, Almighty Allah alone.

In Western society today we hear a great deal of talk about "freedom." Such freedom, Islam asserts, is in reality enslavement; enslavement to one's own ego or to other human beings or their ideas and values. And all enslavement to anything or anyone other than Allah Most High is enslavement to something which is not worthy to be the master of a human being, for only the Exalted Creator and Sustainer of the universe can be worthy of occupying this place in the life of one who has been made (as the Qur'an states) superior even to the Angels. True freedom does not consist of license to do whatever one wants while being the slave of one's own particular deity, rather freedom consists of being free from enslavement to anything or anyone other than one's real Master. Islam's unique task is thus to liberate man from enslavement and servitude to anything other than Allah, and to free him to worship and serve Him alone.

"Say (O Muhammad): 'Verily, my prayer and my worship
my life and death, are for Allah, the Lord of the worlds.
He has no associate (in His divinity). This I am commanded,
and I am the first of those who submit.' Say: 'Shall I seek
for a lord other than god when He is the Lord of all things?
Every soul draws the earning (of its acts) on none but
itself. No bearer of burdens can bear the burden of another.
In the end you will all return to Allah; then He will tell
you about that concerning which you differed.' It is He
Who has made you vicegerents of the earth and has raised
some of you above others in rank so that He may test you
in what He has given you. Indeed, your Lord is swift in
punishment, yet He is indeed the Forgiving, the Merciful."

(6:162-165)

2. The Angels

"But verily, over you are protectors (Angels), kind and
honourable writing down (your deeds)."   (82:10-11)

"He sends down His Angels with inspiration of His
command to such of His servants as He pleases, (saying),
'Warn (man) that there is no god but I, so do your duty to
Me.'"
(16:2)

"The Messenger believes in what has been sent down to
him from his Lord, as do the men of faith. Each one (of
them) believes in Allah, His Angels, His scriptures and
His messengers...."   (2:285)

Belief in the existence of beings called Angels is common to
various faiths. It is also a fundamental belief of Islam. But what,
in the Islamic frame of reference, are Angels?

It is obvious that Allah, the All-Mighty, the All-Knowing, is
able to create any kinds of creatures He pleases. As we can see
within our world alone, He has indeed created an enormous variety
of creatures of all sorts, with very different natures, functions and
appearance, among which are some beings possessing intelligence.
The Holy Qur'an makes it clear that men are not the only
intelligent beings created by Allah.[1] Another order of intelligent

---

1. Yet another species of intelligent beings are *jinn,* who, the Qur'an
    tells us, are made from fire. Like man, they possess freedom of choice:
    some of them are good and others are evil. According to Islam, Satan
    (Iblis or Shaytan) and his kind are *jinn* (not fallen Angels) to whom
    Allah gave leave to try to tempt man, to lure him away from submission

beings are Angels, who act as Allah's agents and serve Him in many ways. They are created of light and unlike men and *jinn* have not been endowed with free will.   Thus they are absolutely obedient to Allah's commands and are engaged in worship and service to Him. They are sent to protect men, to administer Allah's punishments, to carry His messages, and to perform various other functions. Human beings cannot as a rule see or hear Angels, but they are present in our world nevertheless, carrying out the various duties assigned to them by their Creator. Each human individual is attended by two Angels who record all his deeds up to the moment of his death in an account which will be presented to him on the Day of Judgment, the accuracy of which he will not be able to deny.

Because the glory and majesty of the Creator is so awesome and overwhelming that a limited, flesh-and-blood human being is unable to bear direct contact with Him, Allah chose to convey His revelation to the prophets, including Muhammad (Allah's peace and blessings be on them all) through the agency of an angel[2] The name of this honoured angelic messenger is Gabriel (Jibreel) in Arabic.[3] It is because of this vital role of Angels as bringers of the Divine revelation to the prophets that beliefs in them is so important as to form a fundamental article of faith in Islam.

Contd..

and obedience to Him. Thus man must strive throughout his life against "the evil of the whisperer who withdraws, the one who whispers into the hearts of mankind from among *jinn* and among men" (114:4-6). The Qur'an makes it clear that one whose life is centred on Allah can easily repel Satan whose strategy is weak, while one who is in a state of denial or rebellion against Allah is likely to be in Satan's grip, the prey of evil within himself and without.

2. The single known exception to this is the Prophet Moses to whom Allah spoke directly.

3. Gabriel is referred to in the Qur'an as *"ar-Rooh"* (the Spirit). *"Rooh al-Qudus"* (the Holy Spirit). and *"Rooh al-Ameen"* (the Trustworthy Spirit). It is possbile that through some error of understanding the early Christians may mistakenly have taken the Angel Gabriel to be part of the Allahhead, under the influence of the pagan conceptions surrounding them, considering him, as "the Holy Spirit," to be the "Third Person" of the Trinity (see Qur'an 2:253, in which we read: "And We gave Jusus, son of Mary, clear evidence, and We aided him with the Holy Spirit." [*Rooh-al-Qudus,* referring to Gabriel).

3. The Revealed Scriptures

"And before this was the Scripture of Moses as a guide
and a mercy. And this Scripture (the Qur'an) confirms it
in the Arabic tongue, to warn the wrong-doers and as a
glad tidings to those who do good." (46:12)

"And in their footsteps We [1] sent Jusus the son of Mary.....
We gave him the *Injeel*, [2] therein was guidance and light,
and confirmation of what is in hand of the *Taurat*, [3] a
guidance and an admonition to those who fear Allah."
(5:46)

"It is He, Who revealed to Thee (Muhammad) the Scripture
(the Qur'an) in truth, confirming what is in hand of (the
scriptures) that went before it. And He revealed the *Taurat*
and the *Injeel* before this as guidance to mankind. And He
revealed the Criterion (of judgment between right and
wrong)....." (3:3-4)

Belief in the reality of Allah's guidance to mankind in the form
of revealed books or scriptures is another basic article of belief in
Islam.

We have already discussed the Islamic teachings concerning
the oneness and continuity of the Divine guidance throughout the
history of man, that guidance which only the One Who possesses
absolute knowledge of all things could provide for His creatures.
However, the guidance revealed to all the prophets before Muhammad
(peace be on them all) was sent to particular groups of people; it
was not intended to be universal because humanity had not yet
reached the stage of readiness for such a final, comprehensive
statement of Allah's guidance for all time to come. This is clear
from what the Qur'an states concerning the messages given to
various prophets, from what the Old Testament says concerning
them, and from the statement attributed to Jusus that "I was sent
only to the lost sheep of the house of Israel" (Matthew 15:24).

---

1. Allah speaks of Himself in the Qur'an interchangeable as "I," "He"
   and "We."

2. The original scripture revealed to Jusus.

3. The original scripture revealed to Moses.

The final link in the chain of revealed scriptures, Islam asserts, is the Holy Qur'an. *Qur'an* is an Arabic word meaning "reading" or "that which is to be read." It was revealed to the Prophet (peace be on him) over a period of twenty-three years during the interval between his fortieth year and his death in numerous parts which bore an intimate relationship to the events through which the Prophet and his community, the first Muslims, were passing at the time. As we have mentioned, it was communicated to him through the agency of the Angel Gabriel. The Angel appeared to the Prophet on frequent occasions in his true angelic form or in the form of a man during intense states of inner concentration which were at times observed and documented by the Prophet's companions and family members; they have left behind for posterity a clear account, which is confirmed by the Prophet's own narratives, of how the revelations came to him.

The Qur'an speaks in powerful, moving language of the attributes of Allah, His immense power and creativity, of man's relationship and responsibility to Him, and of the certainty of the coming of the Last Day and the Life Hereafter. It lays down moral and ethical principles to govern all aspects of human life, both individual and collective, as well as practical guidelines for various types of human interaction. It also narrates the histories of some of the earlier prophets and people as an example and encouragement to the Prophet and his community, and as a warning to those who deny Allah. Its main theme, reiterated over and over in powerful terms, is the reality of Allah's existence and supreme power, the purposefulness of His creation and of all that occurs, and man's position as Allah's slave, His steward and vicegerent who is accountable to Him in everything.

The Holy Qur'an is the only divinely-revealed scripture in the history of mankind which has been preserved to the present time in its exact original form. For although parts of earlier revelations, such segments of the Torah (*Taurat*) given to Moses, the Psalms (*Zaboor*) revealed to David, and the Evangel (*Injeel*) revealed to Jusus still remain, they are so heavily intermixed with human additions and alterations that it is very difficult to determine what part of them constitutes the original Message (as many Biblical scholars admit only too readily), much less to guide one's life by them. That the Qur'an has been preserved in the exact Arabic wording in which it was revealed to Prophet Muhammad (peace be on him) and in the exact order in which he himself placed it as commanded by Divine revelation, is a matter well-documented historically and beyond dispute.

Because it is the word of Allah, the Qur'an is always recited in Arabic, the language in which it was revealed, in the Islamic prayers (*salat*) and on other occasions, never in translation. However, it may certainly be *read* for understanding in translation by those who do not know Arabic, together with a commentary if desired. Nevertheless, because of its extremely distinctive style and language, it is impossible for a translation to do more than convey its bare meaning. The great nobility of its form of expression, the earnest, moving, eloquent style which is its outstanding characteriztic, cannot be translated, and hence any translation must be regarded (as all translators themselves confirm) as a mere approximation to the sense of the words. While Islam does not rest on miracles or signs and wonders as some other religions do, many who are familiar with the highest in Arabic literary style regard the Qur'an itself as a miracle, so unparalleled is its language and form of expression. Indeed, the Qur'an itself contains a challenge to the unbelievers of Muhammad's time to try to produce a piece of writing comparable to it, and while many tried during his time to compose something similar to it, no one could succeed in doing so. To one conversant with Arabic, the Divine origin of the Qur'an can be readily grasped by comparing Muhammad's language (of which thousands of word-for-word examples are recorded) with the language of the Qur'an, which is the word of Allah. The one is ordinary language of an Arab of his time, while the other is language of such a sublime and exalted quality as no human being has ever been able to approximate either then or since. We will have to say more concerning the Divine origin of the Qur'an under the next topic, the messengers of Allah.

> "And if you (the unbelievers) are in doubt as to what We
> have revealed to Our servant (Muhammad), then produce
> a *surah* (chapter of the Qur'an) like it, and call your
> witnesses besides Allah if you are truthful. And if you

cannot—and you cannot—then fear the Fire (of Hell) whose fuel is men and stones, which awaits those who reject faith."   (2:23-24)

"This is the Scripture in which there is no doubt. In it is guidance for the Allah-conscious, who believe in the Unseen, and are steadfast in *prayer* (*salat*), and spend (in Charity) out of what We have provided for them; and those who believe in what was revealed to thee (Muhammad) and in what was revealed before thee, and are certain of the Hereafter. These are on (the way of) guidance from their Lord, and these are they who will be successful"
(2:2-5).

"But most of them follow only conjecture. Indeed, conjecture does not avail anything against the truth. Verily, Allah knows what they do. And this Qur'an cannot be produced by anyone other than Allah. Rather it is a confirmation of that which is in hand (of earlier scriptures) and a fuller explanation of the Scriptures (Allah's revelations to mankind throughout the ages) wherein there is no doubt from the Lord of the worlds."   (10:36-37)

4. The Messengers of Allah

"For assuredly We sent among every people a messenger (with the command), 'Serve Allah and shun wickedness.' Of them were some whom Allah guided, and of them were some on whom error became inevitably (established). So travel through the earth and see what was the end of the deniers (of truth)."   (16:36)

"Say (O Muslims): 'We believe in Allah and in what is revealed to us, and in what was revealed to Abraham and Ishmael and Isaac and Jacob and the Tribes (of Israel), and in what was given to Moses and Jesus, and in what was given to the prophets from their Lord. We make no distinction between any of them (in believing them all to be Allah's messengers), and to Him do we submit ourselves."   (2: 136, also 3:84-85)

The messengers or prophets of Allah have already been discussed briefly. It is important to note here that the Islamic conception of the role and function of prophethood differs somewhat from that of

Judaism and Christianity. In Islam the word "prophet" (*nabi* in Arabic) does not in any way signify one who prophesizes future events. Rather it denotes one who is very near to Allah through the total surrender of his entire being to Him and who receives revelations from Him which constitute a source of guidance for men. If the revelation is in the form of a written scripture, the prophet is in addition a "messenger" *(rasool)* as well. All the prophets who preceded Muhammad (may Allah's peace and blessings be on them all) were sent with a message of warning and guidance to a particular people. None of their messages was intended to be universal, including that of Jusus, who was commissioned by Allah specifically as a prophet to the Children of Israel, until the last messenger, Muhammad (Allah's peace and blessings be on him) was entrusted with the final and complete statement of Allah's guidance for the whole of humanity for all time to come

Who were some of the prophets of Allah? The Qur'an states that Allah sent a warner and guide to every people, and it mentions the names of many of them. At the beginning of the line was Adam (Adam in Arabic), the first human being. Adam and his wife Eve (Hawwa), originally in a state of primal innocence, exercised the human attribute of freedom of choice and disobeyed Allah's command. Through this they learned the hard lesson of the consequence of disobedience to the Divine command in the loss of their innocent state and life of peace and tranquility. But, the Qur'an states, they repented and Allah forgave them. He then bestowed prophethood upon Adam, giving him guidance for himself and his descendants.

The first true human beings on earth were thus Believers in the One Allah, submitting to His guidance. But gradually over a period of time their accurate perception of Reality deteriorated and they became animists or idolaters, until Allah raised a new messenger among them to recall them to the truth. The Qur'an mentions Noah (Nuh), who brought a message of warning and the need for reform to his totally corrupted people; when they refused to take heed Allah destroyed them in the Deluge. The next major prophet whose history is narrated in the Qur'an is Abraham (Ibrahim). Although he grew up among idolaters, he reasoned out the folly of believing in the divinity of any finite thing, especially of those made by human hands, and he surrendered himself to Allah with such total submission that Allah made him an example for people of all times. The Qur'an calls him "*muslim*," and so indeed all the prophets were *muslims*—that is, those who submit themselves to Allah alone.

From Abraham came a long line of prophets through his two sons, Ishmael (Isma'il) and Isaac (Ishaq). Ishmael was the progenitor of the Arab peoples and Muhammad (peace be on him) was among his descendants. From Isaac came a number of prophets, including his son Jacob (Yaqoob), his grandson Joseph (Yusuf), Moses (Musa), David (Daood), Solomon (Sulayman), John the Baptist (Yahya) and Jusus ('Isa). Of these Moses, David and Jusus (Allah's blessings and peace be on them) brought written scriptures revealed by Allah, although today only scattered portions of the originals remain, intermixed with what people have added, as is clear from an objective study of the format and content of the Biblical text.

Islam asserts that Jusus was one in the line of porphets sent to the Children of Israel. The Message he brought reiterated the necessity of submission to Allah and obedience to His law given through Moses, emphasizing purity of heart and sincerity of intention instead of mere formalism and empty adherence to ritual. The Qur'an states, as does the Bible, that Jusus was born of a virgin mother by the power of Allah. However, this is no way makes him of divine nature or Allah's Son any more than it makes Adam, who was born without the agency of parents, Divine. Jusus was a human being who was created in a special and unique manner by Allah, Who is able to create what He wills as and how He pleases. The notion of the divinity or Sonship of Jusus, the Qur'an asserts, is completely contrary to the true message which Jusus (peace be on him) brought of the Oneness and Uniqueness of Allah, and his insistence that Allah alone—not himself—was to be worshipped and obeyed. (This topic will be discussed in greater detail in coming pages).

Muhammad (may Allah's peace and blessings be on him) was born nearly six hundred years after Jusus (570-632 After Christ) in Makkah, Arabia. He lived at a time when his people were in the grip of the worst form of idolatry and their society was in a state of marked corruption and decay. Within Arabia, Jews had formed tribes and settlements, but they did not propagate the message of the Oneness of Allah and man's responsibility to Him outside their own community. Christianity was splintered into many diverse feuding sects and its stronghold, the Eastern Roman Empire (Byzantium), was in a state of decline.

When, in the midst of this decadent society, a Messenger arose in the city of Makkah with the earnest, burning call to repentance and reform, he issued to the leaders of paganism a challenge which they could not afford to ignore if they were to retain their grip on the people. "Arise and warn" was the message with which Allah charged him. But his warning was met with the most intense hostility. At first he was ridiculed and opposed, and then with his small group of followers progressively exposed to abuse, defamation, torture, boycott and ultimately the threat of assassination. Every means the pagans could devise to induce him to give up his mission and force the early Muslims to abandon Islam was attempted. All of them remained firm and constant, however, for their certainty of the truth of the Message was so strong that the mere threat of physical harm or death could not deter them from believing in it, proclaiming it and living it. Some of the first Muslims died under torture, and other were sent to Abyssinia, a country under the rule of a devout Christian king who subsequently secretly embraced Islam, to escape persecution.

At length, after thirteen years of patient preaching and bearing with constancy all these trials, Allah opened to the Prophet and his followers the possibility of migration to the city of Yathrib (Madinah) some three hundred miles distant, at the invitation of its inhabitants who had embraced Islam; they pledged their loyalty to the Prophet and swore to live and if necessary to die for Islam. In small groups the Muslims left Makkah and made their ways across the desert to the city which had opened its heart to the new faith, and when they had all gone, the Prophet himself, together with his closest friend, Abu Bakr, also left, by Allah's guidance avoiding the pagans attempts to assassinate him in Makkah and hunt him down on his journey.

In Madinah, away from the continuous day-to-day persecutions of the pagan Makkans, the Prophet was able to give form and continuity to the community and system he had been commanded to establish. Here the parts of the Qur'an constituting legislation concerning various matters were revealed, and here they were put into practice by the Muslims as soon as the verses were received by the Prophet. Here the Islamic community and state, with all the various elements of social, political and economic life cast into a form which would be an example for all the future generations of Muslims, came into existence.

But even here there was no peace for the Prophet and his community; they were repeatedly harassed by the continued threats and military expeditions of the pagans, and by the opposition and treachery of dissident groups in and around Madinah. Yet the Muslim community, although initially small in number and poorly-equipped for battle, resisted with such valour that after some nine years it was able to subdue these enemies by a series of actions, both military and diplomatic. The Prophet (peace be on him) then entered the city of Makkah, from which he had migrated several years earlier, as the leader and ruler of a humbled populace. Instead of reproaching or taking any sort of vengeance upon those who had persecuted him so cruelly, he freely forgave even his most bitter enemies, and thus the "conquest" of Makkah took place without bloodshed. The Prophet entered the Ka'aba, the sacred house of Allah's worship built in antiquity by the prophets Abraham and Ishmael, and with his own hands broke into pieces the three-hundred-and-sixty idols which had been erected and worshipped there, purifying the Ka'aba once again for the worship of Allah, the Praised and Exalted, alone.

Prophet Muhamamd (Allah's peace and blessings be on him)[*] died about a year later. Truly he had delivered the Message with which he had been entrusted by Allah. and he left behind for all time to come two permanent, unchangeable sources of guidance: the Holy Qur'an and his *Sunnah*—that is, his own example and practice, the details of which were within some years collected in many well-documented verbal reports known as *Hadiths* which have been presented accurately to the present time as the second source of guidance in Islam after the Qur'an.

After the Prophet, four of his closest friends and companions—
Abu Bakr, 'Umar, 'Uthman and 'Ali—became the leaders and
heads of the Muslim society and state with the title *Khalifat
Rasool Allah*, that is, caliph or successor to the Messenger of
Allah. They ruled scrupulously according to the guidance of the
Qur'an and the Prophet's example. After them, however, the
political leadership took the form of a hereditary monarchy which
deviated markedly from the example of the Prophet and the first
four Rightly-Guided Caliphs. At the same time, Islam spread with
great rapidity, carried to many parts of the globe by the Muslims
whose individual lives and societies had been transformed by their
faith. At its zenith (700 to 1600 after Christ) the Islamic Empire
reached from Spain to the Philippines, and, at a time when Europe
was still in a very primitive state, the light of faith, learning and
culture which illuminated Muslim lands was truly the beacon of
piety and civilization in an otherwise darkened world.

The Qur'an is emphatic in proclaiming that Muhammad (peace
be on him) is the last messenger of Allah, the "Seal of the
Prophets," and that any who claim prophethood after him are
false. But why, it may be asked, if Allah had sent messengers to
earlier peoples as the need arose, and as man's course on this
planet is not yet run and the need for guidance is so evident today,
should there be no further prophets after him?

This is so because the Qur'an is Allah's final and complete
guidance for all humankind. As such it does not require any
amendment, abrogation or restatement. Moreover, it was revealed
at a time when man's intellect, consciousness and the ability to
preserve and transmit knowledge through writing had reached full
maturity. The Qur'an has been preserved, word for word, letter for
letter, exactly as it was revealed, and as long as it remains so (and
the Qur'an contains Almighty Allah's promise to safeguard it from
alteration until the Last Day), there is no need for any further
revealed guidance. The Qur'an is complete and perfect, and its
principles and teachings are as valid and bindings today as at the
time when they were revealed; for although the style and mode of
human life have changed, the Ultimate Realities, the nature of
good and evil, and man's own nature are unalterable and permanent
verities which are in no way affected by the passing of time or
changes in the human condition.

Besides this, there is another reason why no further messengers are needed. Supplementing the guidance set forth in the Qur'an is the example of the Messenger, Muhammad (peace be on him). A divinely-revealed Book might contain Allah's guidance, but a Book was not enough; someone was needed to translate that guidance into action, to *live* it. And that someone was not to be an angel or a super-human being but a man like other men, a man from among the community to which the guidance was immediately addressed, who would serve as a living example to others and would give concrete form to the laws which Allah had revealed amidst the varied conditions of ordinary human existence.

Concerning the life of the Prophet (peace be on him), such a complete and detailed account has been preserved as has probably not been kept concerning any other individual in human history. Because of the absolutely unique position he occupied as the recipient of revelations from Allah, the Praised and Exalted, every act and detail of his life was of greatest interest to those around him. Hence the narrations preserved in the books of *Hadith* (sayings of the Prophet) deal with all facets of his life, from the most personal matters to the conduct of war and the affairs of state. Consequently Muslims have before them in every aspect of their lives—and it is to be borne in mind that in the Islamic frame of reference no part of man's existence is outside the pole of religion— the living example of the best of human beings. As his wife 'Aisha said concerning him, his conduct *was* the Qur'an. And while Muhammad (peace be on him) was an individual of immense spirituality and nearness to Allah, at the same time he also lived an extremely full, active and complete life, exemplifying many varied and complex roles. He was a devoted husband, father and grandfather, a kind and responsible kinsman, a faithful, affectionate friend, a leader alike in worship and battle, a ruler and statesman *par excellence*. For the Muslims of his time as well as for the Muslims of today and tomorrow, he was and is and will always be the model: the teacher, the guide, the leader, and above all the conveyor of the Divine guidance, the connecting link with Allah, and the person whom they love, revere and emulate above all other men.

"You have indeed in the Messenger of Allah a beautiful
pattern for any whose hope is in Allah and the Last Day,
and who engages much in the praise of Allah." (33:21)

"O Prophet, truly We have sent thee as a witness, and a
bearer of glad tidings and a warner, and as one who
invites to Allah by His leave, and as a lamp spreading
light. Then give the glad tidings to the Believers that they
shall have from Allah a very great bounty." (33:45-47)

Now there have been many claimants to prophethood, some
even in modern times. How, therefore, can anyone prove that
Muhammad's claim to be a messenger of Allah, to have received
Divine revelation, is true? In short, could Muhammad actually and
in fact have been the Messenger of Allah, the Last Prophet, or did
he merely imagine he was or pretend to be?[1]

The real question being asked is, in fact, how can one distinguish
a true prophet from a false one? In order to determine the truth of
any person's claim to have brought a divinely-revealed scripture,
it is necessary to establish some rigorous criteria which are
generally acceptable in terms of logic and reason. These criteria
should be such that in the light of them anyone may searchingly
examine any scripture, whether it is the Qur'an, the Old and New
Testaments, the Bhagavad-Gita or any other religious text, and
decide for himself whether or not it deserves serious consideration
as coming from the Lord of the universe. Such criteria may be
something like the following:

1.   The person claiming to have received revelation should be
known as an individual of unblemished character and morals, of
whom no evil or sin is known; in particular he must be of the
strictest standard of honesty and truthfulness.

---

1.   It is perhaps very difficult for many of us, in this age of loss of spiritual
     values and lack of spiritual individuals, to imagine or even believe in
     the possibility of a human being good enough to be a prophet. Yet even
     today among the devout Muslims, there do exist individuals who are so
     absolutely pure in heart and in conduct, so deep in faith and so near to
     Allah, that although they are still far from approaching the character of
     a prophet, they nevertheless make it possible to understand that such
     a person, totally surrendered to Allah and submitting to Him with the
     entirety of his being, could and in fact did actually exist.

2.   The words of the alleged scripture should be recorded exactly as they were received from the Divine Source, without the slightest interference or change on the part of anyone, including the one who claimed to have received the revelation. The original scripture should remain intact and accessible to anyone who wishes to read it.

3.   The message contained in the scripture should be totally consistent throughout; no part of it should contradict any other part.

4.   There should be no confusion among it concepts and teachings.

5.   Nothing in it should be contrary to the objectively-observed facts of the natural world.

6.   It should appeal to man's reason and rational faculties rather than to irrationality, superstition and the like.

7.   It should provide spiritual insight and moral guidance of the highest order.

8.   It should not attribute to Allah anything which is contrary to His unique, exalted and transcendent nature, nor to any created being anything which pertains exclusively to Allah.

9.   It should emphatically deny to anyone other than Allah the right to be worshipped and obeyed.

10. It should emphasize Brotherhood and equality among human beings, and should not uphold the domination of some people by others.

11. It should not attribute major sins or vices to the persons whom Allah singled out for the task of conveying His guidance (the prophets), for this is tantamount to attributing lack of knowledge or stupidity to Allah.

12. Its language should be eloquent and sublime, and of the highest order of literary style and expression.

13. Although it is not essential as a proof of its truth, if it contains objectively-verifiable information such as could not be known by anyone other than the Creator, it will be considered a further testimony to its truth and genuineness.

If the reader should be interested in carrying out such an examination of the Qur'an, it is important that he approach it with a completely open mind, uncoloured by earlier preconceptions or prejudgments about Islam and its Books. It is also suggested that he begin his reading of the Qur'an from the far end rather than from the beginning, or, if he plans to read bits and pieces rather than the whole of it, to open it anywhere he pleases at any point in his reading. The reason for this is that the Qur'an is not a volume with the sequential order of a conventional book, and thus it may be opened and approached from any portion or page. The most powerful and moving *surahs* (chapters) are by and large found in the latter portion of the Book, while the long *surahs* near the beginning contain considerable matter dealing with legislation, the early Muslim community, relations with non-Muslims, the histories of earlier prophets and their peoples, and various other subjects. It is also suggested to use a translation by a Muslim rather than by a non-Muslim, as it is likely to be more accurate and true to the spirit of the Arabic,[2] and, if possible, one containing a commentary for clearer understanding.

From such an examination of the Qur'an, we can make the following important points:

1. We observe that Muhammad brought a Message over a period of twenty-three years which, from the first revelation to the last, was totally consistent with itself, without any contradiction, confusion or change.

2. The wording of the existing Qur'anic text (of which there is only one standard Arabic version throughout the world) remains word-for-word exactly as Muhammad received it, and its verses

2. An exception to this is the translation by A.J. Arberry. A list of the better translations will be found among the list of recommended books at the end of this volume.

ard sections are in the exact order in which he himself placed them as commanded by Divine revelation.

3.   We observe that the language of the Qur'an is completely different from the speech of Muhammad, which has been recorded in his exact words in the voluminous collections of *Hadiths*, and that it has a unique, sublime, exalted quality which is also different from the speech of any human being before or since, which even the enemies of the Prophet, despite their most strenuous efforts, were unable to imitate.

4.   The concept of Allah and of the Ultimate Realities which the Qur'an expresses is of the utmost degree of fitness and sublimity, as are the spiritual truths and moral guidance it sets forth.

5.   Muhammad did not know how to read or write, nor was he learned in any branch of knowledge. Although he may have had some idea about the basic teachings of Christianity and Judaism, his knowledge of these religions cannot have been more than quite superficial. However, the Qur'an contains innumerable references to these religions, their teachings and the histories of the earlier prophets in such depth and detail as could not possibly have been mastered by anyone who was not literate and of a very high degree of religious knowledge. In addition, other elements of the Message he brought are such that it would have been impossible under any circumstances for an illiterate Arab of his time either to master or to construct them within his own mind—impossible, indeed, for any human being of any time or place, for, a great part of them relate to *al-Ghaib*, the Unseen Realities, containing information which can be known only to the Creator of all things.

6.   Not only does the Qur'an contain nothing which is contrary to reason or objectively observed fact, but it repeatedly appeals to man to use his reason and logical faculties to verify the truth of its message. In particular, it cites example after example from the natural world as a proof of Allah's limitless power and wisdom. In addition to this, it also contains matter related to the world of nature which was not known or understood by anyone until many centuries later. Here are only three examples:

"Do those who disbelieve not see that the heavens and the earth were of one piece, then We parted them? And We made every living thing of water. Will they not then believe? And We placed in the earth firm hills lest it quake with them, and We placed therein ravines as roads that they may find the way. And We have made the sky a roof withheld (from them), yet they turn away from its signs. And it is He Who created the night and the day and the sun and the moon. They float, each in an orbit."

(21:30-33)

"And Allah created every animal from water. Among them is that which goes upon its belly and among them is that which goes on two legs and among them is that which goes upon four. Allah creates what He wills. Verily, Allah has power over all things."   (24:45)

"Verily, We created man from a quintessence of wet clay, then placed him as a drop in a safe lodging. Then We made the drop a clot. Then We made the clot a lump, then We made the lump bones, then clothed the bones with flesh, and then produced it as another creation. So blessed be Allah, the best of creators."   (23:12-14)

These verses, which first came to light in sixth century Arabia, are so extraordinary that it is worthwhile to study them very closely. Was there anyone in Muhammad's time who had the remotest inkling of the processes by which the universe came into being, or that all life, and every form of animal, originated from water, or of the balancing force which mountains provide to the earth, or the fact that the heavenly bodies all "float" along "in orbit"? For views less heretical than these the scientists of Europe were called to account by the Inquisition centuries later. Or was there anyone during his time who understood the detailed stages and processes by which a drop of sperm becomes a human infant? And these are not stray examples. The Qur'an is full of statements concerning the natural world which totally conform to modern scientific findings, some of which could not have been understood in scientific terms by anyone until fairly recent times.[3] Moreover,

---

3. For an elaboration of this see *The Bible, Qur'an and Science*, by Maurice Bucaille, American Trust Publications. Indianapolis. 1978.

the Qur'an exhibits an extraordinary depth of insight into human nature, particularly in relation to the contrasting states of mind of one who is deeply grounded in faith in Allah and one who is in a state of disbelief or rebellion against Him. In this it outshines the most subtle contemporary researches into human psychology, dwelling on the state of peace, balance, direction and contentment of the believer on the one hand, and the iner emptiness, anxiety depression and confusion of the nonbeliever on the other.

7.   Finally, we note that the man who brought this scripture was renowned among his people for his faithfulness, good character and honesty. He was so respected for his truthfulness and upright character that his fellow Makkans had honoured him with the title of *"al-Ameen"* (the Trustworthy) years before the beginning of his call to prophethood. He repeatedly warned others with utmost urgency of the enormity of attributing anything to Allah, whose displeasure he feared more than anyone because of the immensity of the responsibility which had been laid upon him, from their own minds or imaginations. Could such a man, then, have been the forger, over a period of more than two decades, of a scripture which he claimed was revealed to him by Allah but which was actually of his own fabrication?

In view of all the foregoing, one is left with only two possible explanations of the scripture called the Qur'an: either that Muhammad really was what he claimed to be, the individual to whom Allah Most High had entrusted the awesome task of conveying His ultimate guidance to mankind, or that he was the most outrageous and flagrant liar and deceiver who ever lived; and this is so totally at variance with everything that is known about him as to be absolutely impossible. But even if we accept for a moment for the sake of argument the possibility that Muhammad made up the entire Qur'an over this long period of time, we are still left without any explanation of how even the most audacious forger could have had knowledge of the many matters in the Qur'an which it is absolutely impossible that any human being of his time could have known or even remotely imagined, how the whole Qur'an could be so utterly consistent and free of contradiction, of such sublime depth and inimitable language, and how it could have such a convincing, unassailable, earnest ring of truth in its exposition of the Ultimate Realities.

Some have tried to explain away the Qur'an by alleging that Muhammad was mad or epileptic. But has there ever been, in all of human history, an instance of a person in the grip of epileptic seizures, insanity or any other form of mental aberration producing anything so consistent and coherent, of such profound depth and wisdom, something which was beyond the knowledge of any human being and which was beyond the capacity of the sanest and wisest men to produce?[4] The pagan Makkans of Muhammad's own time, trying their utmost to avoid coming to grips with the truth of what he brought, tried in vain to explain away his Message by similar allegations, and by claiming that he must be in the grip of poetic frenzy, or a soothsayer or one possessed; they even suggested that someone learned in Christian doctrines must be teaching him. But Muhammad had no knowledge at all of composing poetry, nor did he have any of the well-known bizarre characteriztics of a soothsayer or a man who is possessed. As for the "teacher" theory, it could not be carried very far with a man who was always in the full view of his enemies as well as of his followers (who both, for their own individual reasons, scrutinized with utmost care every detail of his life), and who often received the Divine revelations in their presence. Hence these charges were soon dropped, and even his most implacable enemies were forced to come to the conclusion that what he was receiving was indeed, as he claimed, from Allah. Moreover, he asked nothing for himself. No one can debate the fact that he had nothing whatsoever to gain and everything to lose—his life itself—by persisting in his mission in the face of the relentless persecutions of the pagans; while if his aim had been to achieve fame, power or wealth (the only possible motivations which can be ascribed to him if his Message was not what he claimed), the pagan Makkans did in fact offer him all these and would gladly have given them to him instantly to deter him from proclaiming his revolutionary statement of man's

4.   See Abdul Hameed Siddiqui, *The Life of Muhammad*, Islamic Publications. Lahore, Pakistan, 1975, pp. 59-63, and Zakaria Bashier. *The Meccan Crucible*, FOSIS, London, 1978, pp. 83-104, for a discussion of this point.

accountability to Allah and the Brotherhood and equality of all Muslims which threatened to destroy the entire edifice of their power, prestige and decadent life-style.

Consequently, if we return to the Message and look at the sublime concepts and ideas it embodies; its total consistency from beginning to end; the lofty standard of morality and human interaction it lays down; its profound, self-evident wisdom and depth; the extremely noble, earnest, moving quality of its tone and language; and what it contains relating to matters not then known to any human being on earth (least of all to an illiterate Arab) concerning the physical universe as well as the Unseen Realities, it becomes impossible to ascribe the Qur'an to human authorship. As a result, having ruled out every other possible explanation for the phenomenon of the Qur'an, we are compelled to conclude that it is, as Muhammad (peace be on him) proclaimed, the word of Almighty Allah. In the words of the Qur'an itself:

> "So I swear by all that you see and all that you do not see that this is verily the speech of an honoured messenger (Gabriel). It is not the speech of a poet; little is it that you believe. Nor is it the speech of a soothsayer; little is it that you remember. (This is) a revelation from the Lord of the worlds. And if he were to invent any sayings concerning Us, We would assuredly seize him by his right hand and cut off his life-artery, and not one of you could keep Us from him. And verily, this is a reminder for the Allah-conscious. And We surely know that some among you will deny it, and that it is indeed a source of sorrow to the unbelievers. But verily it is the truth of assured certainty. So glorify the name of thy Lord, the Almighty."
> (69:38-52)

> "And thus have We, by Our command, sent inspiration to thee. Thou didst not know (before) what revelation was and what faith was, but We have made it (the Qur'an) a light with which We guide such of Our Servants as We will, and verily thou guides to the straight way—the way of Allah, to Whom belongs whatever is in the heavens and whatever is on earth. Behold (how) all affairs tend toward Allah."
> (42:52-53)

"This Qur'an is not such as can be produced by anyone
other than Allah, but it is a confirmation of earlier revelations
and a detailed explanation of the Scripture (the totality of
Divine guidance since the beginning of man's history on
earth) in which there is no doubt from the Lord of the
worlds.   (10:37)

Then what about the claims made by other "prophets," of
either ancient or modern times, that they, too, received revelation
from Allah and perhaps a scripture? Again, we must go to the
messages they brought and examine them carefully in the light of
stringent criteria such as those suggested earlier for determining
the truth of a scripture. Next we carefully examine the lives of the
"messengers" themselves to see whether they conform to any sort
of an accepted standard of righteousness and purity, intelligence
and credibility.[5] Then if the claimants to prophethood of either
ancient or modern times do not meet such criteria as we may
consider to be an objective and valid test of truthfulness and
credibility, we are forced to regard their claims as fabrications and
those who brought them as deliberate forgers and deceivers of
their fellow-men. In many passages the Qur'an speaks of the
terrible punishment which will come to those who invent lies
against Allah, as in the following:

"And who does more wrong than one who fabricates lies
concerning Allah or who says: 'I receive revelations', when he
does not receive revelations at all, or who says, 'I will reveal
the like of what Allah has revealed'? And if thou couldst see
when the wrong-doers are in the pangs of death and the Angels
stretch out their hands, (saying), 'Render up your souls. This
day are you recompensed with the punishment of degradation
because of what you spoke about Allah without truth and
because you scorned His signs.'"   (6:93)

5. Islam holds that a prophet possesses the following characteriztics: he
   is absolutely truthful; he is free of any kind of major sins: he delivers
   the message with which he has been charged without any failure or
   concealment; and he is of the highest order of intelligence and mental
   ability. Obviously if those who claim prophethood do not possess such
   essential qualities. Almighty Allah can be accused of ineptitude in His
   selection of the people to whom He has entrusted the most important
   task on earth!

And it is up to every human being to use the intelligence Allah gave him to determine the credibility of such claims for himself, for truth and falsehood are two different things and each can be recognized by its own special characteriztics.

5. The Hereafter

"Verily We shall give life to the dead, and We record all that they send before and that they leave behind, and We have taken account of all things in a clear Book (of evidence)."   (36:12)

"And to every soul will be paid in full (the fruit) of its deeds, and He knows best all that they do."   (39:70)

Belief in the Hereafter—what pertains to the Day of Judgment, bodily resurrection, and Heaven and Hell—is another basic article of faith in Islam.

As we have already seen, Islam asserts that the present life is but a minute part of the totality of existence. The Qur'an informs man of the reality of another Life of a very different nature from the life of this world, of infinite duration. For Allah, the All-Wise, All-Powerful Creator, is able to do anything He pleases, and He is easily able to transform His creations from one state of being to another. Can we for a moment imagine that it can be more difficult for Almighty Allah to raise us up when we are dead than it was to create us in the first place? The Qur'an speaks again and again of familiar and obvious examples of such transformations: the coming to life again of the earth after it lies dead and barren in the grip of winter or drought; the development of a sperm and an ovum into an embryo in the environment of the mother's womb, and its further development from that state into a thinking, feeling, acting human being living in the world.

"And among His signs is this: Thou seest the earth barren and desolate, but when We send down rain to it, it is stirred to life and yields increase. Verily, He Who gives life to the (dead) earth can surely give life to the dead. Lo! He has power over all things."   (41:39)

"O mankind! If you are in doubt concerning the Resurrection, then, verily, We created you from dust, then from a drop, then from a clot, then from a lump of flesh (both) shaped and shapeless, that We may make it clear for you. And We cause what We will to remain in the wombs for an appointed time, and afterwards We bring you forth as infants; then you attain your full strength. And among you there is he who dies (young) and among you there is he who is brought back to their most abject time of life so that, after knowledge, he knows nothing. And thou seest the earth barren, but when We send down water on it, it thrills and swells and puts forth every lovely kind (of growth). That is because Allah is the Reality, and it is He Who gives life to the dead, and it is He Who has power over all things, and because the Hour (of Judgment) will come concerning which there is no doubt, and because Allah will raise those who are in the graves." (22:5-7)

"Does not man see that it is We Who created him from sperm? Yet behold, he is an open adversary. And he makes comparisons for Us, and forgets his own creation. He says: 'Who can give life to bones when they are decomposed?' Say: 'He will give them life Who created them the first time, for He knows about every kind of creating." (36:77-79)

"Then how can you reject, faith in Allah, seeing that you were without life and He gave you life? Then He will cause you to die and will bring you to life again and again to Him will you return." (2:28)

As we have seen, Islam lays the greatest stress on the individual's accountability to Allah. The human being's life in this world constitutes a trial, an examination period during which he prepares himself, either for good or for ill, for the next Life of infinite duration. The Day of Judgment may be compared to the ending of the examination, during which the Teacher will ask each individual student, "What were you doing during the exam?" and will then evaluate the work he hands in. For although man's body dies, his soul, his personality has an existence extending beyond the present life; it is a continuous entity whose inner state will accompany it into the Hereafter. It is this state together with one's deeds, which will determine one's ultimate destiny.

It is obvious that an individual who has lived with the correct awareness of and relationship to Reality through submission to Allah Most High is in an entirely different inner state from one who has lived all his life with an incorrect or distorted awareness of Reality and in forgetfulness, rebellion and ingratitude vis-a-vis Allah, and who has died in this state. Moreover, although many of the deeds of such people may appear outwardly similar, they have been motivated by entirely different intentions: the one to obey and please Allah and the other for any reason other than pleasing Allah, Whose reality he does not acknowledge. Indeed, the difference between the inner states of such persons is so great that their being kept apart from one another, in entirely different environments corresponding to what is within them and among companions having a similar inner condition, is a requirement of the most rudimentary conception of justice, not to speak of the absolute, unswerving justice of All-Knowing, All-Wise, Infinitely Just and at the same time Most Merciful Allah.

In very vivid, awe-inspiring language, the Qur'an sketches over and over the outline of the events of the Last Day. At a time when Allah sees fit, which is known only to Him, this world will be brought to an end in a terrifying cosmic cataclysm frightful beyond imagination. And on that awesome Day of Judgment, the bodies of the dead will be raised from their graves and rejoined with their souls, while those who were alive on earth at that time will die and be joined to this assembly. All men, past and present, will then stand before Allah, each one as totally alone and helpless as when he came into the world, to render their accounting:

> "When the sky is rent asunder and attentive to its Lord in fear, and when the earth is flattened out and has cast forth all that was within it and become empty, and attentive to its Lord in fear. O thou man! Verily thou art ever labouring on labouriously toward thy Lord, and thou shalt meet Him. Then he who is given his Record in his right hand will surely receive an easy reckoning and will return to his people joyfully. But as for him who is given his Record behind his back, he will invoke destruction and will be thrown to scorching Fire. Verily, he lived among his people happily; truly he did not think that he would have

to return (to us). Nay, but lo! his Lord was watchful of
him. So I do swear by the ruddy glow of sunset, and by the
night and what it envelopes, and by the moon when it is
at the full, you shall surely travel from stage to stage."
(84:1-19)

"Then when there comes the deafening noise, that Day a
man shall flee from his brother and his mother and his
father, and his wife and his children. Each one of them
that Day will have enough concern (of his own) to make
him indifferent to the others. Some faces that Day will be
becaming, laughing, rejoicing. And other faces that Day
will be dust-stained; blackness will cover them. Those
will be the deniers of Allah, the doers of iniquity."
(80:33-42)

Then those who denied Allah and rejected His guidance, who
devoted themselves to the worship of deities other than Allah, and
who did evil deeds will be consigned to a fearsome and terrible
abode in which their companions will be others who, like themselves,
are completely alienated from Allah. There they will be in a state
of enduring torment and agony from which will be no respite. They
will long to have another chance to return to the world to live their
lives differently in the light of their present knowledge of Reality
but it will be too late; the examination will be over and all the
bcoks closed, and they will have no choice but to acknowledge the
justice of their destiny which is due to what their own hands
wrought, in spite of all the clear warnings which were sent to guide
them.

"And on the Day those who disbelieve will be placed
before the Fire, (they will be asked). 'Is not this real?'
They will say, 'Yes, by Our Lord.' He will say, 'Then
taste the punishment because you disbelieved.'" (46:34)

"Verily, the sinners will be in the punishment of Hell, to
remain therein. It will not be lightened for them and they
will be overwhelmed in despair. And We shall not be
unjust to them, but it is they who have been unjust to
themselves."   (43:74-76)

As for those who believed in Allah, who obeyed and submitted to Him and lived their lives for His pleasure, and who left this life in a state of surrender to Him, a state of unutterable contentment and satisfaction awaits:

> "O My servants, no fear shall be on you that day nor shall you grieve—those who have believed in Our signs and submitted. Enter the Garden, you and your wives, in rejoicing."　　　　　　　　　　　　(43:68-70)

> "Those who believe and do righteous deeds, they are the best of creatures. Their reward is with their Lord: Gardens of Paradise beneath which rivers flow. They will dwell therein forever, Allah will be pleased with them and they with Him. This is for those who hold their Lord in awe."
> 　　　　　　　　　　　　(88:7-8)

These two states, Heaven and Hell, will be experienced in physical form by the new bodies with which Allah will raise men up; they are not merely spiritual or psychic states. And while we do not know their exact nature, the Qur'an tells us that the inhabitants of Heaven will experience some things which will remind them of their life on earth, that the happiness and beauty of it will far exceed anything one can imagine, and that the ultimate triumph and bliss for those who have attained Paradise will be in nearness to their Lord. As for those who have deserved Hell, theirs will be a temporary or permanent state of torture depending on their inner condition and the nature and extent of their sins. The Qur'an describes Hell as a state of intense, fearful burning and agony without respite, among the most horrifyingly loathsome surroundings and companions. But the Most awful part of the suffering of its inhabitants will be the terrible, inescapable awareness that this is the destiny which they deserved and brought upon themselves by rejecting Allah and ignoring the guidance which He had conveyed to them through His messengers.

This clear reality of the future Life is always before the mind and consciousness of the devout Muslim. It is this awareness which keeps the present life, in the midst of the most intense happiness and the deepest pain alike, in perspective: the perspective of a passing, temporary abode in which one has been placed as a test in order to qualify and prepare himself for his future Home. This perspective is essential for the maintenance of mental balance and stability amidst the difficulties of life. Yet no Muslim, even the best among them, imagines that he is guaranteed Paradise; on the contrary, the more conscientious and Allah-fearing one is, the more he is aware of his own shortcomings and weaknesses. Therefore the Muslim, knowing that Allah alone controls life and death, and that death may come to him at any time, tries to send on ahead for his future existence such deeds as will merit the pleasure of his Lord, so that he can look forward to it with hope for His Mercy and Grace.

"When the sky is cleft asunder, when the stars are dispersed, when the oceans burst forth and the graves are overturned, a soul will know what it has sent ahead and kept back. O man, what has made thee careless concerning thy Lord, the Bountiful, He Who created thee, then fashioned thee and then proportioned thee? In whatever form He wills, He casts thee. Nay, but they deny the Judgment. And verily, over you are guardians (Angels), generous ones recording; they know all you do. Verily, the righteous ones will be in bliss, and verily, the wicked will be in the Fire. They will enter therein on the Day of Judgment and will not be able to keep away from it. And what will convey to thee what the Day of Judgment is? Again, what will convey to thee what the Day of Judgment is? A day when no soul shall have any power whatsoever for (another) soul. The command that Day will be (wholly) with Allah."

(82:1-19)

"The likeness of the life of this world is as the rain which We send down from the sky. By its mingling arises the produce of the earth from which men and animals eat. (It grows) until, when the earth is clad with its ornaments and is decked out, and its people deem that they are the masters of it. Our command comes to it by night or by day, and We make it like a clean-mown harvest as if it had not flourished yesterday. Thus do We explain the signs (of Allah) for people who reflect. And Allah calls to the Abode of Peace He guides whom He pleases to a straight path. To those who do right is a goodly (reward) and more (than that). No darkness nor shame shall cover their faces. These are the people of the Garden; they will abide therein. But those who have earned evil will have a reward of like evil, darkness will cover them. No protector will they have against Allah, as if their faces had been covered with pieces from the depths of darkness. They are the people of the Fire; they will abide therein."

(10:24-27)

6. The Divine Decree

"What Allah grants to men out of his mercy, no one can withhold, and what He withholds no one can grant apart from Him. And He is the Powerful, the Wise." (35:2)

"No misfortune can befall on earth or in yourselves but is recorded in a Book (of Allah's decrees) before Allah brings it into existence." (57:22)

The final article of faith in Islam is belief in Allah's decree. This is known in Arabic as *Qada wa qadar,* meaning the "measure" what is ordained by Allah and His "plan."

Since the entire scheme and plan of creation is under the direction and control of the Almighty Creator and Sustainer, everything that is or that happens in the universe, from the smallest to the greatest events, is governed by Allah's will, an integral part of His eternal plan. Nothing can take place without His ordaining it, nor is there such a thing as a random, chance event.

Perhaps the meaning of this' can best be illustrated by an example. To many people the miraculous events which are reported in the Qur'an or the Bible, or the possibility of revelation from Allah to mankind, may seem unimaginable, mere superstition or fables because, according to their understanding of Reality, "Allah does not intervene in human affairs;" the same sort of argument is often used and has been since the beginning of time—to justify man's disbelief in the guidance brought by the prophets, the Afterlife, and so on. The Muslim, on the other hand, possesses the clear certainty that Allah is absolutely real and that He is continuously active in all of His creation, including the world of men. All that exists or takes place, therefore, is the expression of His will, from the behaviour of each atom of matter to the large-scale occurrences of human history to events of cosmic proportions. And since all of it is His, determined by His permission and decree, nothing that happens can ever be understood as "intervention" or "supernatural," or as a random, chance even devoid of meaning and purpose, whether it happens in the world of nature or in the world of men. In human life, ease and suffering alike, and the events which produce them, equally have a purpose and meaning, and are equally a part of Allah's infinitely wise plan for His creation.

Such a belief gives the Muslim a tremendous degree of inner certainty, confidence and peace of heart, especially in the face of afflictions, for he knows that since everything is under the control of the All-Wise, Most-Merciful Allah, the circumstances of his life are likewise under His control and direction, and hence are not without a reason and a purpose. Moreover, he lives with the assurance that whatever is to come to any individual, including death, cannot fail to come at its appointed time nor is it to be withheld by any means, while conversely, nothing which Allah has not decreed for him can be brought about by any means whatsoever

This inner certainty frees the Muslim from fear of anyone or anything other than Allah, for he knows that no one has the slightest power either to injure or to benefit him without His leave. If Allah decrees some good for him, no one can keep it away, and at the same time, if He decrees some harm for one, no one has the power to avert it except Him. The Qur'an expresses this very succinctly:

> "Say: 'Who guards you in the night or in the day from the Merciful?' ... Or do they have gods who can shield them from Us? They cannot help themselves nor can they be defended from Us.'"   (21:42-43)

And the Prophet (peace be on him) said:

> "When you ask anything ask it from Allah, and if you seek help seek help in Allah. Know that if the people were to unite to do you some benefit they could benefit you only with what Allah had recorded for you, and that if they were to unite to do you some injure they could injury you only what Allah had recorded for you.   (Hadith)

For Allah alone is the source of benefit or harm, and turning to anyone or anything other than Him for protection and help when everything "other" is itself dependent on His will is not only utterly futile but wrongfully attributes to others powers which Allah alone possesses, thereby distorting the accurate perception of Reality.

In any situation, Islam teaches the task of a human being is to make a sincere effort, to strive, to do his best—not, as is so often incorrectly stated, simply to sit back and let things take their course in blind resignation to some supposed "fate" or "destiny": for a human being does not know and cannot know wherein his destiny lies, and until he has exhausted all possible means and what is inevitable occurs, he cannot be said to have encountered that destiny. But then whatever Allah decides, whatever comes to one after all his efforts have been made, should be received with patient and trustin acceptance of what He in His infinite wisdom has seen fit to send, and with the expectation that it may prove to be a source of good and of ultimate blessing in the broader perspective of the Life-to-Come.

Belief in the Divine decree is thus a statement of belief in the meaningfulness and purposefulness of all that is, and essential part of the Muslim's sense of total trust; dependence and submission in relation to his Creator. We will have more to say concerning this subject in later pages.

On these basic beliefs, then, the Islamic faith rests:

the Oneness of Allah (Allah);
the scriptures revealed by Him for the guidance of mankind;
Allah's messengers, the prophets;
the Angels, His emissaries and agents;
the Hereafter: the Day of Judgment, the resurrection, and the states of Heaven and Hell; and
Allah's all-wise, all-powerful decree.

> "The Prophet believes in what has been revealed to him from his Lord, and so do the Believers. They all believe in Allah. His Angels, His scriptures and His messengers, making no distinction among His prophets. And they say, 'We hear and we obey. Grant us Thy forgiveness, our Lord, and unto Thee is the journeying.'"　　(2:285)

ACTS OF WORSHIP

Central to the Islamic teachings and way of life are various obligatory acts of worship *(ibadat)* which are often referred to as the "Five Pillars of Islam." These consist of (1) the declaration of faith. "I bear witness that there is no deity except Allah and I bear witness that Muhammad is the Messenger of Allah," (2) the prescribed prayers, (3) fasting during the month of Ramadan, (4) the poor-due, and (5) the pilgrimage to Makkah.

While the aim of each to these acts of worship is the remembrance and glorification of Allah Most High, it must be emphasized that Allah's majesty and glory do not depend in the slightest degree upon the praise or even acknowledgement by His creatures, for He is absolutely independent of His creation and free of all needs; rather it is man who needs these recurrent forms of worship to keep his contact with his Lord and his vision of the true Reality clear and strong. The purpose of the Islamic worships is, therefore, to strengthen the individual's faith and sense of submission to Allah, to solidify his character, to discipline him for his role as Allah's faithful servant and steward on earth, to make it possible and easy for him to live in the manner ordained by Allah, and to reinforce the ties of Brotherhood and affection among Muslims.

As will be seen in the following sections, these acts of worship require the participation of all aspects of man's nature—his soul, his mind, his feelings and his body with its various needs and appetites, and his time, energies and possessions as well—and thus they are the worship by the *total* human individual of Allah Most High. It will also be seen that the various forms of worship are prescribed at various time intervals. For example, the declaration of faith is to be always present in the mind and heart of the Muslim and to be uttered again and again with the tongue during his daily prayers. The prayers are to be performed five times daily every day of one's life after attaining puberty, and even more often if one desires to strengthen his relationship with Allah further and come nearer to Him. Fasting is for a full month every year, while the poor-due is to be calculated and paid once yearly, and the pilgrimage is to be performed once in a lifetime if possible (the latter two are obligation only on those Muslims who meet certain required conditions, as will be seen presently). These two aspects of the Islamic worships—the involvement in them of the total human being and the prescription of them at different recurring intervals—make them extremely unique and complete expressions of man's total dependence upon Allah and submission to His will, his utter humility and creatureliness before the greatness of the Creator, and his desire to serve and obey Him alone.

These acts of worship are obligatory upon all Muslims no matter where they may happen to live, whether they are institutionalized in a Muslim society or one happens to be a single Muslim living far away form any Muslim community. It is the collective obligation of Muslims to provide the means and facilities for carrying out these duties faithfully. Each of these acts of worship is prescribed in the Holy Qur'an, and each is performed in the manner in which the Prophet (peace be on him), who is the example for all Muslims of every time and place, himself performed them.

In this section we will discuss the concepts and significance of the various Islamic worships. The details of how they are carried out have been left for a later section in the context of the daily life of Muslims, with the exception of the pilgrimage which, for the sake of coherence and continuity, has been presented in entirety in the present section.

1. Declaration of faith (*Shahadah*)

> "Islam is based on five things: the testimony that there is no deity except Allah and that Muhammad is His slave and Messenger, the observance of prayer, the payment of the poor-due, the pilgrimage, and the fast during Ramadan."
>
> *(Hadith)*

The first of the acts of worship is to believe with the heart and declare with the tongue that there is no deity except Allah and that Muhammad is the Messenger of Allah. This is expressed in the words *"Ashaduan la ilaha illa Allah wa ashaduanna Muhammadan Rasool Allah"* (I bear witness that there is no deity except Allah and I bear witness that Muhammad is the Messenger of Allah).[1]

Here, as we saw earlier, the word "deity" is used in the broad sense which the Arabic word *ilah* conveys: that is, anyone or anything who is worshipped, to whom one's love and devotion are given and one's goal is directed; it also denotes that Being in Whom is vested ultimate authority and the right to prescribe and legislate, Whose words or commands are considered binding, and Who alone is worthy to be obeyed. Thus it becomes clear that this declaration has a far broader meaning than the words convey in English. It is, in effect, a proclamation that the one who believes and utters it cancels from his heart, loyalty, devotion, obedience, submission to and worship of anything other than Allah, the Praised and Exalted—not merely of man-made idols of wood or stone, but also of any conceptions, ideologies, ways of life, desires, loves, preoccupations and authority-figures which claim his supreme devotion, loyalty, obedience and worship.

Similarly, *"Muhammadan Rasool Allah,"* although it is a very brief, terse statement, denotes a whole train of thought beyond the mere words as they are rendered into English. This proclamation of belief in Muhammad as Allah's Messenger is simultaneously a proclamation of belief in the guidance which that Prophet (peace be on him) brought to mankind—Allah's final and complete guidance for all humanity—and at the same time implicitly a statement of the intention to faithfully follow that guidance.

---

1.   An alternative wording used interchangeably with the above is "... *wa ashaduanna Muhammadan abduhu wa Rasooluhu"* (... and I bear witness that Muhammad is His slave and Messenger). This denotes that even Muhammad, the best and most perfect of all men, was, like all other human beings, Allah's humble slave. This makes it clear that the terms "slave" and "messenger" are complementary, not contradictory, because the greatest of prophet is, in spite of his exalted station among his fellow human beings, just as much as the humblest of men or the worst of sinners, Allah's slave, albeit the most honoured among all the slaves of Allah.

2. Prayer *(Salat)*

"And be steadfast in prayer *(salat)* and regular in poor-due *(zakat)*, and whatever good you send forth your souls before you, you shall find it with Allah. Verily, Allah sees all that you do."   (2:110)

"O you who believe, seek help in patience and *salat*. Verily, Allah is with those who patiently persevere." (2:153)

"What stands between a man and disbelief is the abandonment of *salat*."   *(Hadith)*

The second act of worship which Islam prescribes is the performance of prayers *(salat)* within certain established time periods five times a day.

Why have prayers been prescribed for Muslims five times a day? it may be asked. Would not once or twice, or whenever one happens to feel like it, be sufficient? In answering these questions, it must first be pointed out that the Islamic prayers *(salat)* are somewhat different from "prayer" as used in the Christian sense, although personal supplication and glorification of Allah (known as *du'a*) are also a very important part of the Muslim's worship in addition to *salat*. Actually, the word "worship" conveys the meaning of *salat* much more accurately than "prayer"; accordingly we have retained the word *salat* wherever possible in order to maintain this distinction.

Basically *salat* consists of recitation from the Holy Qur'an and glorification of Allah accompanied by various bodily postures. The five times of worship correspond to the five periods of the day: daybreak, noon, afternoon, the close of day, and night, corresponding to the organization of man's time around various activities. Keeping all this in mind, we can now proceed to answer the above question of "why?"

Salat is a multi-faceted act of worship. Performing it regularly serves as a repeated reminder to the Muslim during the day and night of his relationship with his Creator and his place in the total scheme of Reality. Its purpose is to keep him from ever forgetting that he belongs not to himself or even to the people who are closest to him but to Allah, and that he is His slave, obedient to His command. The remembrance of Him and glorification of Him for a brief, concentrated period in the midst of his daily activities keeps this perspective always clear and intact. No matter how faithful or conscientious an individual may be, such reminders are essential, for man's involvement in his human concerns and activities is so engrossing that it is very easy to lose sight of one's relationship with Allah, his place in the total scheme of things, his responsibilities, and his ultimate goal. The world around us is full of example of persons who, while they may be well-intentioned, have clearly forgotten who they are in relation to the total Reality and what their ultimate destiny will be.

This is achieved in part by the recitations from the Qur'an which are a part of every prayer.[1] These bring to mind not only the basic Islamic teachings concerning Allah, man, the universe and the Hereafter, but they also recall the Muslim to his obligation to Allah, to other people and to himself, for as the Qur'an says, "*Salat* restrains from shameful and unjust deeds" (29:45). This continuous reminder keeps the conscience alive and functioning in a proper manner; without the reconditioning it undergoes by the regular performance of *salat*, it is likely to become estranged from its Source, inactive and easily corrupted. It will be obvious that prayer once a week or even once or twice a day simply does not fulfill this purpose and is moreover only a partial and very inadequate expression of the human creature's relationship with his Sustainer Who, in the words of the Qur'an, is "nearer to him than his jugular vein." (50:16)

In addition to this, through the bodily postures of the prayer, which consist of standing, bowing, prostrating and sitting, repeated a specified number of times in each prayer, the Muslim expresses submission, humility and adoration of Allah Most High with his

---

1. As stated previously, Muslims always recite the Qur'an in Arabic during *salat*, whether they are Arabic-speaking or not. A new convert to Islam who does not know Arabic may recite verses in translation in his/her own language until able to memorize at least two short passages in Arabic, which is generally fairly easy for most people to do.

entire being. The heart which is filled with the love of Allah, the consciousness of its own creatureliness and Allah's greatness and beneficence, indeed has an urge to express of all these feelings in physical as well as verbal form. By means of *salat*, which enlists the participation of man's total nature, Islam provides the means of expression, in an extremely dignified and moving form, for these needs and feelings.

Indeed, the self-discipline which is needed to perform *salat* regularly and at the proper times — to perform the ablution which precedes the prayer, and to carry on these prayers in the early morning when sleep is so attractive, during the busy daylight hours when one is preoccupied with work, family and other activities, and at night when one is tired and wants to relax or sleep—reaffirms the human being's total dependence on his Creator and his position as His slave. *Salat* is truly the complete expression of man's voluntary submission to Him. *Salat* is so important in maintaining this attitude of submission that it is obligatory even during any type of illness (certain modifications have been permitted to those who are ill, travelling or fighting in battle). And it is to be performed with strict concentration, attention and presence of the heart, not simply as a mechanical, verbal and physical exercise. *Salat* and its significance to the devout Muslims are best described in the inimitable language of the Qur'an."

> "Verily, in the creation of the heavens and the earth, and the alternation of night and day there are signs for men of understanding—those who remember Allah standing and sitting and lying on their sides, and ponder over the creation of the heavens and the earth, (saying): Our Lord, Thou has not created this in vain. Glory be to Thee! Then save us from the punishment of the Fire. Our Lord, indeed the one whom Thou admittest to the Fire Thou coverest with shame, and for the wrong-doers there will be no helpers. Our Lord, we have heard the call of one calling us to faith: "Believe in your Lord," and we have believed. Our Lord, then forgive us our sins and blot out from us our iniquities, and take us to Thee among the righteous. Our Lord, grant us what Thou didst promise us through Thy messengers, and do not shame us on the Day of Judgment, for indeed, Thou dost not fail in Thy promise."
> (3 190-194)

A Muslim is required to pray at the prescribed times wherever he may be — whether in a mosque, in his home, at work, or in any other clean environment indoors or outside — but it is preferable and more meretorious to pray in congregation with his fellow-Muslims if possible. In such a congregational prayer, in which Muslims stand in straight rows shoulder to shoulder as one body united in the worship of Allah, the elements of discipline, orderliness, Brotherhood, equality and solidarity are very strongly exemplified. Non-Muslims who are seeing Muslims pray in congregation for the first time are often very much struck by this living expression of Brotherhood, equality and discipline.

Because of all these aspects, *salat* is the principal means whereby the Muslim keeps his life in correct perspective, having always before his mind the limited, finite nature of this world's life, with all its allurements and involvements, pleasures and pains, and tne certainty of death and the Life-to-Come, attempting to maintain a sense of balance and proportion between the needs and claims of this world and the Hereafter. Through worship at regular, fixed intervals marking the periods and divisions of the day, the individual voluntarily affirms the relationship existing between himself, the slave, and his Master, Allah Most High, acknowledging and maintaining Allah's rights and claims on him in the midst of his involvement with his worldly affairs.

> "Allah is the Light of the heavens and the earth. The similitude of His light is as a niche wherein is a lamp. The lamp is in a glass; the glass is as it were a shining star, kindled from a blessed tree, an olive neither of the East nor of the West, whose oil is almost luminous although no fire has touched it. Light upon light! Allah guides to His light whom He wills, and Allah draws up parables for mankind, for Allah is the Knower of all things. In the houses in which Allah is exalted and in which His name is remembered there are people who glorify Him at morning and evening—men whom neither merchandise nor trade takes away from the remembrance of Allah and constancy in *salat* and payment of *zakat,* who fear a Day when the hearts and the sight will be overturned; that Allah may reward them with the best for what they have done and increase the reward for them out of His bounty, for Allah provides for those whom He wills without measure."
>
> (24:35-38)

3. Fasting *(Sawm)*

"O you who believe, fasting is prescribed for you as it
was prescribed for those before you in order that you may
be conscious of Allah . . . Ramadan is the (month) in
which the Qur'an was revealed as a guide to mankind and
as a clear evidence for guidance and judgment (between
right and wrong). So whoever among you witnesses this
month, let him spend it in fasting; but if anyone is ill or
on a journey, the prescribed period (should be made up)
by days later. Allah intends ease for you and He does not
intend hardship, and (He desires) that you should complete
the prescribed peroid, and that you may glorify Allah for
guiding you and that you may be thankful."(2:183-185)

Fasting is a practice common to many religions. Islam has also
prescribed fasting for Muslims in the form of a month- long period
of abstinence accompanied by intensive devotional activity which
constitutes the third of the obligatory acts of worship.

Islam establishes a lunar calendar in which the months are all
either twenty-nine or thirty days long. The ninth month, Ramadan,
is the month in which the first revelation of the Qur'an came to the
Holy Prophet (peace be on him). The fast of Ramadan has been
prescribed in order to train Muslims in self-discipline and scrupulous
obedience to Allah's commands; it is not related to penance for
sins or regarded as a means of appeasing Allah's wrath as in some
religions. Again, in distinction to the fasting of some religions, the
fast of Ramadan involves *total* abstinence from all food, drink and
marital relations throughout the daylight hours; not even water
may be taken. However, the fast must be broken at sunset each
day, and it is also recommended to have pre dawn meal before
resuming the fast the next day!

In addition to refraining from meeting these ordinarily-lawful
necessities, Muslims also engage in increased devotional activity
throughout this month. Besides the usual five prayers, an additional
salat called *taraweeh*, which is observed only during Ramadan,
is performed either individually or in congregation each night. It
is, more over, a *sunnah* (practice) of the Prophet (peace be on him)
to complete the recitation of the entire Qur'an during Ramadan,
and many present-day Muslims follow this tradition. The last ten
days and nights of Ramadan are marked by especially intensive
devotions, including the commemoration of the night during which
the first revelation of the Qur'an came to the Prophet, known as the

Night of Power. Giving Charity is especially enjoined during Ramadan, and restraining the tongue and temper are an additional aspect of fasting.

Fasting makes the Muslim discipliend, steadfast and resilient like a soldier who forgoes or postpones the satisfaction of his normal needs at the order of his Commander. This trains him to be flexible and adaptable in his habits, capable of enduring hardship, and not to take for granted the bounties of Allah which he normally enjoys. Fasting also enables the Muslim to feel with the poor who daily experience hunger, and to be active in compassion and Charity toward them.

Islam recognizes that physical needs and appetites, particularly those of food, drink and sex, are powerful factors in human life, tying man to dependence on and preoccupation with his bodily needs and desires. Hence the Muslim is asked for one month out of the year to do without the satisfaction of these needs by day in order to develop his spiritual nature. The process of experiencing hunger, thirst and sexual abstinence—of imposing them on oneself voluntarily, so to speak—has the effect of weaning a human being away from dependence on physical satisfactions and the dominance of his animal needs, freeing him to pursue spiritual goals and values during this period. Ramadan is thus a month, out of the twelve months of the year, during which the Muslim, due to the lack of his usual involvement with his physical needs, has a unique opportunity (which of course depends on his own initiative to utilize or forgo) to devote himself to Allah and to his spiritual development.

While such fasting may sound difficult to those who are not used to it, in practice it is generally tolerable and even easy for most people; in fact, it appears to have some therapeutic and beneficial effects on the body which are not yet clearly understood in scientific terms. Indeed, Muslims often become so accustomed to the altered routine of Ramadan and experience such an intense spiritual life during it that when it ends they feel a poignant sense of loss and wait eagerly for the next Ramadan to attain the same high spiritual level again, carrying its experiences and lessons with them throughout the coming year.

At the conclusion of Ramadan, Muslims celebrate one of the two major festivals of Islam, the 'Eid al-Fitr, the Festival of Fast-

Breaking. This occasion, as well as the practical details of fasting, will be discussed under "The Islamic Way of Life."

4. Poor-Due (*Zakat*)

> "It is not righteousness that you turn your faces toward the East or the West, but righteousness is that one believe in Allah and the last Day and the Angels and the Book and the prophets; and (that he) give his wealth, out of love for Him, for kinsmen, orphans, the needy, the traveller, those who ask, and to ransom captives; and (that he) establish salat and give zakat. And those who keep their commitments when they make them and are patient in tribulation and adversity and in the struggle: they are the truthful and they are the Allah-conscious." (2:177)

The Arabic word *Zakat*, which literally menas "purification," has no actual and precise English equivalent; the term nearest to it in meaning is "poor-due." *Zakat*, the fourth of the acts of worship in Islam is thus the Muslim's worship of Allah by means of his wealth through an obligatory form of giving to those in need.

Islam proclaims that the true Owner of everything is not man but Allah, Who bestows wealth on people out of His beneficence as He sees fit. Hense those to whom He has given more have an obligation to spend from His bounty for their brothers or sisters who need help. In concrete terms, *zakat* consists of an amount which is assessed on the nonessential property of the Muslim, to be distributed among:

> "The poor and the needy, and those who work on it (collecting *zakat*), and those whose hearts are to be reconciled,[1] and (to free) captives and (help) debtors, and in the cause of Allah, and for travellers." (9:60)

In addition to helping individuals who are in need or distress, *zakat* funds may also be spent (as mentioned above) "in the cause of Allah," i.e., for the construction of mosques, religious schools and hospitals, and for the salaries of those involved in the propagation or study of Islam whose work keeps them from having time to earn a livelihood.

---

1. This refers to converts to Islam who are in material difficulties for one reason of another after embracing Islam.

Zakat is not to be paid on property which is for personal use (for example, clothing and household furniture, a house in which one lives, a car one drives, crops planted for domestic consumption) but is assessed at approximately 2-1/2 per cent per year on cash or capital which is beyond one's immediate needs, as, for example, cash savings or investments, the inventory of a business, cattle, lands and crops which are a source of profit, and so on. *Zakat* is to be paid once a year and is assessed on property only after a full year has passed since its acquisition and after any debts or other legitimate obligations have been met. Each Muslim's *zakat* is calculated individually, depending on the amount of "*zakat-able*" wealth or property he possesses and varying from year to year.

But why should this precribed poor-due be called a "purification"? This is so because, since all wealth in fact belongs to Allah Who gives it in trust to people as He sees fit, a part of what one possesses is to be returned back to Allah in this form. The Qur'an speaks of the obligation of *zakat* in very moving words:

> "Verily, the Allah-conscious will be in the midst of gardens and springs (in the next Life), taking that which their Lord gives to them. Indeed, before that they were doers of good. They would sleep but little at night and in the early dawn they would pray for forgiveness, and in their wealth (was remembered) the right of him who asked and him who was prevented (from asking, although needy)." (51:15-19)

Hemce the payment of *zakat*, which is the share of Allah and the Muslim community in the Muslim's wealth, purifies his remaining possessions and makes his ownership of them legal and permissible. It also purifies his heart from greed and selfishness, and from regarding what Allah in His bounty has bestowed on him as solely his by right. In turn *zakat* purifies the heart of the one who receives it from envy and hatred of others who are better-off. Rather than being his enemies or exploiters, the affluent are his brothers-in-faith who acknowledge his right on what Allah has given them and, from His bounty, extend their help to him. The obligation of *zakat* has been mentioned repeatedly in the Qur'an in the same sentence as the obligation of *salat* to underscore its being a fundamental duty of a Muslim, a prescribed act of worship. In fact, the first caliph of Islam, Abu Bakr Siddiq, sent an armed force against a group of people who refused to meet the obligation of *zakat* while observing *salat* and professing to be Muslim.

When practiced as prescribed, *zakat* is thus in effect a form of social security in the Muslim society. In prescribing this obligation, Almighty Allah assuredly did not intend to make people lazy and expectant of receiving handouts; indeed, it is preferable to give *zakat* to one who does not ask, and it is to be given only in the amount that meets the most basic needs, not for purchasing non-essentials. But in any society there will always be people in distress and want for one reason or another: due to some calamity, war, a disabling condition, the inability to find work, or orphans, widows and the aged who are unable to work and who have no one to provide for them. Obviously there must be some permanent, workable provision for these which is also compatible with human dignity and which simultaneously eliminates bitterness and envy between the rich and poor. *Zakat* is thus an institutionalised, obligatory kind of sharing and caring which equalizes the wealth in the community without, at the same time, banning private ownership of property or stipulating that all people must possess an equal amount of wealth, which is contrary to human nature and to dynamism and development within a society. It is to be remembered that *zakat* was instituted fourteen hundred years ago. In spite of all the modren advances in economic systems, methods of distribution of wealth, and concern for the rights of human beings to have thier basic needs met, no ideology or economic system has been able to develop any institution comparable to *zakat* for dealing with the problem of poverty while at the same time offering a solution to class rivalries and hatreds.

Besides the payment of the obligatory *zakat*, Islam also urges Muslims to give voluntary Charity, to the extent they can afford, to those in need. Indeed, charitableness is among the most stressed qualities in Islam. A Muslim is supposed to be always responsive to human need and distress, and to regard his wealth as a trust from Allah which is to be used not only for himself and his family but for other human beings in need as well.

> "You will not attain righteousness until you spend out of that which you love. And whatever you spend from (your) possessions, indeed Allah is aware of it."   (3:92)

"They ask thee (Muhammed) what they should spend.
Say: 'whatever you spend that is good is for parents, the
near of kin, orphans, the needy and the traveler, and
whatever good you do, surely Allah knows it....' They ask
thee what they should spend. Say: 'What is beyond your
needs.'"   (2:215,219)

5. Pilgrimage *(Hajj)*

"And (remember) when We prepared for Abraham the
site of the (Sacred) House, (saying): 'Do not ascribe
anything as associate with Me, and sanctify My House for
those who circumambulate it and those who stand and
those who bow and those who prostrate themselves (there).
And proclaim the *hajj* to men; they will come to thee on
foot and (mounted) on every kind of lean camel coming
through deep ravines.'"   (22:26-27)

"The first house (of worship of Allah) appointed for men
was that at Bakka,[1] full of blessings and of guidance for
all kinds of beings. In it are signs manifest: the station of
Abraham—whoever enters it attains sanctuary. Pilgrimage
to it is a duty men owe to Allah—those who can afford the
journey...."   (3:96-97)

Hajj—that is, pilgrimage to Makkah in Saudi Arabia—constitutes
the fifth and last of the acts of worship prescribed by Islam.
Obligatory once in a life-time for those Muslims who can afford
it provided there is safety and security for travel and that provision
is left behind for dependents, *hajj* constitutes a form of worship
with the totality of the Muslim's being: with his body, mind and
soul, with his time, possessions and the temporary sacrifice of all
ordinary comforts, convenience and tokens of status and individuality
which human beings normally enjoy, to assume for a few days the
condition of a pilgrim totally at Allah's service and disposal, His
slave who seeks only His pleasure.

Hajj takes place during the first days of the lunar month of

---

1. The ancient name for Makkah.

Dhul-Hijjah, with its climax on the ninth of that month.[2] The rites of *hajj* centre on complete submission and devotion to Allah. At the same time they commemorate as an example of such total submission and obedience Prophet Abraham set especially in his willingness to sacrifice what he loved most in the world—his son Ishmael—at Allah's command   (Holy Qur'an 37:99-113).[3]

People often wonder what Muslims do during their pilgrimage, what *hajj* is actually like. What follows is a brief description of the principal rites and experiences of *hajj* and their meaning to a Muslim

Pilgrims come for *hajj* from all parts of the globe—from the Middle East, Southeast Asia, Africa, Europe, the Americas, even from Australia. The majority of them come by plane to Jiddah, Saudi Arabia's major seaport which is about forty-five miles west of Makkah. Others arrive in Jiddah by ship, and still others travel by bus or private cars from neighbouring countries such as Turkey, Iraq, Iran, Jordan, Syria, Lebanon, Kuwait and other Persian Gulf states, as well as from various parts of Saudi Arabia itself.

As the pilgrims approach Makkah, at places designated by the Prophet himself where pilgrim facilities have been constructed, they enter into a state of consecration known as *Ihram*. *Ihram* signifies divesting oneself temporarily of all marks of status and individuality to assume the humble dress and condition of a pilgrim devoted wholly to Allah. One takes on *Ihram* by expressing his or her intention to enter into that state, making ablution or taking a shower, and putting on the pilgrim's dress (which is also

---

2. On the following day, Muslims throughout the world observe one of Islam's two major feasts, 'Eid al-Adha. On this occasion it is *sunnah* to slaughter an animal (which is also one of the observances of *hajj*) in commemoration of Prophet Abraham's sacrifice of a sheep in place of his son.

3. Although the Old Testament (Genesis 22:1-2) refers to Isaac as the object of the intended sacrifice, the error in this account is made clear by the fact that it refers to Isaac as Abraham's "only son," when it is an historic fact that his son Ishmael was born several years before his son Isaac.

called *Ihram*). The dress of male pilgrims is a garment unique to *hajj*, consisting of two pieces of white, unsewn cloth which cover the lower and upper parts of the body. Although no specific garment is prescribed for women, they also enter *Ihram*, wearing any garment which conceals the shape and covers them completely, leaving only their faces and hands exposed. Pilgrims in *Ihram*, male or female, are to abstain from marital relations, the use of perfume, quarrelling, abusiveness and obscenity. They are also prohibited to harm any living thing, plant or animal (with the exception of dangerous insects, snakes etc.) in the territory of Makkah, which, since the time of Prophet Abraham (peace be on him) has been designated as a sanctuary for all creatures. Pilgrims may, however, engage in all other lawful activities, such as eating and dinking, sleeping, washing, purchasing the necessitites, and so forth.

The pilgrim's first obligation when he arrives in Makkah, after he has found his accommodation and taken care of his physical necessities, is to visit the Ka'aba and perform certain prescribed acts of worship following the example of the Prophet (peace be on him). Now just what is the Ka'aba?

Often referred to as the Sacred House (*al-Bait al-Haram*), the Ka'aba is a small rectangular stone structure[4] which stands inside the compound of the Sacred Mosque (*al-Masjid al-Haram*) in the centre of the city of Makkah. The Ka'aba was originally built in antiquity by Prophet Abraham and his son Ishmael, also a prophet (peace be on them both), as the first sanctuary on earth dedicated to the worship of the One Allah. The story of the building of the Ka'aba is related in the Qur'an thus:

> "And remember Abraham and Ishmael raised the foundations of the (Sacred) House, (saying): 'Our Lord, accept it from us, for Thou art the All-Hearing, the All-Knowing. Our Lord, make us those who submit to Thee and of our descendants a people who submit to Thee. And show us our rites, and forgive us. Indeed. Thou art the Forgiving, the Mercy-Giving.'"   (2:127-128)

---

4. The Ka'aba is approximately 45 feet high, 33 feet wide and 50 feet long.

And again,

> "Remember We made the House a place of gathering for
> men, and of security. And you take the Station of Abraham[5]
> as a place for prayer. And We covenanted with Abraham
> and Ishmael that they should sanctify My House for those
> who circumambulate it or use it as a retreat, or bow or
> prostrate themselves (there in worship)." (2:125)

During the three thousand years since it was first built, the
Ka'aba was demolished several times by natural disasters or the
hands of men, but each time it was rebuilt at the same site and for
the same purpose.[6] The celebrated Black Stone, thought to be a
meteorite, is known to be a part of the original structure; it is set
into one corner of the Ka'aba and, following the Prophet's example,
the pilgrim kisses, touches or points to it while he makes his
circumambulations of the Ka'aba as a gesture of love and respect
for the significance of the Sacred House of Allah. The Ka'aba is
draped with a woven black covering embellished with Qur'anic
verses embroidered in gold; this covering is replaced annually with
a new one.

Because of its unique significance as the first house of worship
of Allah, Islam prescribes that Muslims face the direction of the
Ka'aba whenever they perform *salat;* this direction of the Ka'aba
from any place on earth is known as the *qiblah.*[7] Hence millions

---

5. This refers to a spot adjacent to the Ka'aba where Abraham worshipped.

6. Although the central purpose of the Ka'aba was always acknowledged
   to be the worship of Allah, for a time, beginning long before the birth
   of Prophet Muhammad, it was the centre of the idolatrous worship of
   the pagan Arabs. Inside it stood a vast number of idols which were
   worshipped together with Allah. When the Prophet gained the final
   victory over the Makkans, he demolished the idols and the Ka'aba was
   again restored to its original sacred purpose, that of worship of
   Almighty Allah alone.

7. Many people think, incorrectly, that Muslims always face the East
   when they pray. In fact, they face the direction of the Ka'aba wherever
   it may lie from the place they are in. In most of the United States and
   Canada, this direction is north-east. Although this might appear strange
   at the first glance, if a string is stretched over a globe it will be readily
   apparent that the *shortest* distance from most of North America to
   Makkah is in a north-easterly direction rather than south-easterly as
   one might suppose.

of Muslims in every part of the globe turn their faces toward the same central point five times a day as they offer their worship to Allah. Since at all times some people in some parts of the world are engaged in *salat*, the cycle of worship with its focus toward the Sacred House continues uninterrupted. The Ka'aba is the visible symbol of Allah's Unity, representing in concrete form His centrality in the life of the Muslim, the focal point for Muslims of all times and places to turn toward in their worship as a symbol of their unity as one community submitting to the One Allah, a part of the endless stream of worshippers facing and circling around it unceasingly since remote antiquity in the glorification of Allah Most High.

For the Muslim, visiting the Ka'aba, whether it is for the first or for the tenth time, is a profound, awe-inspiring experience. The worshipper enters the Sacred Mosque by one of its doors, with a supplication for Allah's peace and blessing. Looking beyond the throng of pilgrims and the patterns of columns and arches into the vast open courtyard around which the mosque is constructed, he catches a glimpse, with a tremor of awe and excitement, of the solitary black-draped Ka'aba which is the centre of every Muslim's world. After performing a brief *salat* of "greeting" of the mosque, he makes his way toward the Ka'aba through the vast array of Muslims of every place and race on earth[8] in order to perform the first of the pilgrim's rites, that of *tawaf* or circumambulation.

Seeking out the corner of the Ka'aba in which the Black Stone is embedded, from which the circumambulation is to start, with words of praise to Allah the worshipper joins the host of Muslims circling the House and pouring out their hearts in supplication to Him A sense of timelessness sweeps over him as he realises that he is one atom in an endless ocean of those who have worshipped at this House since nearly the beginning of recorded history. Moving in that sea of worshippers within the shadow of the Ka'aba, a deep sense of his smallness and insignificance comes to

---

8. The number of worshippers in the Sacred Mosque of course depends upon the season. During *hajj* it accommodates hundreds of thousands of Muslims. On other occasions, for example, during Ramadan, on the two 'Eids and on Fridays, it is also very crowded, while at other times the numbers are far less.

him, and all the trappings and defenses of his ego fall away as he realises that Allah alone is great and that none of His slaves can bring any of his worldly props and privileges with him to confront the glory and majesty of his Lord. Here, under the blazing sun of Makkah, making his circuits around Allah's Holy House as he repeats the solemn, moving supplications of the pilgrim, he comes face to face with his own nothingness, his creatureliness, his utter dependence on his Creator in the face of Allah's ineffable glory and sanctity, grasping, in that brief yet intense encounter with the sublimity of Allah, that all the movements and efforts which men make on this earth are as nothing. They and he will pass away, and then he will come alone before the One who gave him his life to receive His judgment and the recompense for all he did.

After completing seven circuits of the Sacred House, the pilgrim may spend as much time as he wishes in making supplications to Allah in the immediate vicinity of the Ka'aba, and before he leaves he prays two *rak'ats of salat*. He will then probably go to the spring of Zamzam, situated underground within the compound of the Sacred Mosque very close to the Ka'aba,[9] to refresh himself with its water. He then goes to a nearby area within the compound of the Sacred Mosque to perform the next rite of *hajj*. This is known as *sa'i*, that is, "hastening" between the two small hillocks of Safa and Marwah, separated now by a long, marble-lined corridor, in commemoration of Hagar's hurried search for water at this site.

While the circumambulation of the Ka'aba centres around

9. Islamic tradition holds that Abraham brought his wife Hagar (Hajirah) and son Ishmael to the barren valley of Makkah, then a desolate, uninhabited spot surrounded by stark lava hills, and left them there at Allah's command. When their supply of water was exhausted and the child began to cry with thirst, Hagar began a hurried search for water, running back and forth seven times between two small hillocks. Her search proved futile but when she turned back to her son. Allah revealed to her the spring of Zamzam flowing at his feet. It has flowed continuously since that time. The presence of water in the midst of the inhospitable desert attracted settlers to the spot which in time became the city of Makkah. In later years Abraham together with his son Ishmael built the Ka'aba very close to the spring.

Allah Most High, the centre of the drama of *sa'i* is man. *Sa'i* is symbolic of man's efforts and movements in this life, of the human soul's ceaseless striving in his journey though the world, together with the host of his fellow human beings. The worshipper walks, and during part of the way may break into a run, seven times between the two lava-rock mounds, situated about a quarter of a mile apart, glorifying and supplicating Allah. Between the marble arches he catches glimpses of the adjacent courtyard of the Sacred Mosque. At the centre of it, like a luminous jewel, stands the black-draped Ka'aba around which, like an endless river flowing on and on day and night since remote antiquity supplicants from every corner of the world, clad in the simple pilgrim's dress, move in utter absorption with Allah, uttering His praises and calling on His name. One who has visited the Sacred House leaves it with an intense longing to return to it again and again, and with a vivid understanding of why the Ka'aba is indeed the focal point of the earth for the worship of Allah, the Praised and Exalted representing in concrete form His centrality in the life of the Muslim individual and community.

Pilgrims may arrive in Makkah to perform their *tawaf* and *sa'i* either immediately before the days of *hajj* or earlier, as they wish; in fact, thousands of pilgrims arrive in Makkah days or weeks before the immediate period of *hajj* in order to have more time to spend in devotion at the Sacred Mosque. However, the climax of the *hajj* occurs on the ninth day of Dhul-Hijjah, the Day of Arafat. The Prophet (peace be on him) stressed the essential nature of this day's observance by saying that one who had been present at 'Arafat would have performed *hajj*, signifying that even if a pilgrim arrived too late to perform the initial rites at the Sacred House, still, as long as he had taken part in the assembly at 'Arafat, his *hajj* would be accepted by Allah.

'Arafat is the name of a vast, empty plain some miles outside Makkah; it is treeless and barren, without any shelter from the blinding desert sun and encircled by stark, jagged purple-black lava peaks. It is to this plain that the entire assembly of pilgrims, over time million in number, moves during the morning of the 9th of Dhul-Hujjah in order to spend the afternoon up to sundown engaged in penitence and supplication to Allah. The pilgrims come by private cars, by buses and on foot, in wave upon wave an unbelievably vast gathering of human beings of amazing diversity, reciting in unison the fervent, moving pilgrim's call of response to his Lord. Thousands of tents are erected on the plain for this occasion to shelter them.

After the noon and afternoon prayers have been performed together in the shortened form recommended for travellers and people have had a chance to eat and rest, the period of devotions begins. During the afternoon up to sundown, all these human beings, assembled here from every land and belonging to countless races and cultures, are completely absorbed in supplication to Allah Most High, glorifying Him, affirming their utter helplessness and dependence on Him, and yearning for His forgiveness and His pleasure, enduring all the fatigues and difficulties of travel and the pilgrimage itself, with its severe climate and hard conditions, for the sake of that intense, profound experience of pouring out their souls before their Lord. The vast, otherwise-empty plain is filled with tents and with thousands upon thousands of pilgrims, tired and disheveled and totally humble before their Creator, standing with hands raised in supplication, many weeping in the intensity of their awe and devotion to Him. Some climb up the Mount of Mercy, a hill in the middle of the plain from where the Prophet (peace be on him) delivered his last *hajj* address to his people, to make their supplications. The gathering of 'Arafat brings vividly to mind the immense gathering of that awesome Day when men's bodies will be brought out of their graves and rejoined with their souls and all will stand in utter humility before Allah Most High to await His judgment, a time when no soul will have anything to bring with it before Allah except its inner state and whatever little good it may have been able to do in this quickly-passing life.

As soon as the sun sets, the exodus of the pilgrims from 'Arafat begins; they go as they came—by bus, car or on foot—in an endless stream which continues for many hours. Their next station is Muzdalifah, a barren, inhospitable, lava-rock wasteland a few miles closer to Makkah, where they perform the sunset and night prayers together, spending part of the night resting after the fatigues of the day and engaged in supplication to Allah. Here they also gather a number of pebbles to be used for stoning three stone columns representing Satan which have stood since ancient times in the village of Mina, to which all the pilgrims go after their brief halt in Muzadalifah, to live for the next two-and-a-half or three days in a vast tent city before they complete their pilgrims' rites and disperse.

These stone pillars stand at the sites where Satan appeared to Abraham and Ishmael (Allah's peace and blessings be on them) in remote antiquity, tempting them to disobey Allah when Abraham was taking his son to be sacrificed at Allah's command. On each of the three days of sojourn in Mina, countless numbers of pilgrims go to the columns, stoning them with the pebbles they have collected to symbolize their rejection of Satan, in a stirring drama of the endless human struggle against evil promptings and temptations.

After the first day's stoning, the pilgrim may shower and return to his ordinary dress, and most of the prohibitions applying in the state of *Ihram* are now lifted. At this time, following the Prophet's example and injunction, many of the pilgrims slaughter an animal in commemoration of Abraham's sacrifice of a sheep in the place of Ishamel; part of the meat is used to feed themselves and their group, and the rest is distributed among the poor. During this period the pilgrims also return briefly to Makkah to perform their final circumambulation of the Ka'aba. The pilgrims' home during the days in Mina is a tent shared with other pilgrims of the same sex or with his family, within specified camp compounds provided by pilgrim guides or by various governments or organizations; he spends the time in making daily trips for the stoning, praying and reading the Qur'an, listening to talks about various aspects of Islam, visiting with his fellow-pilgrims, or resting. Before sundown on the third day or the following morning he leaves Mina and his pilgrimage is now complete.

In addition to its unique spiritual aspects, *hajj* is also remarkable, as we have seen, for the fact that it brings together from every part of the earth such an immense diversity of human beings, who, in spite of vast differences of culture and language, form one community *(ummah)*, all of them professing and living by the same faith and all devoted to the worship of their single Creator. One can see pilgrims from Turkey, from Indonesia, from India; Egyptians and Afghans, Tunisians and South Africans, Malaysians, Saudis, Iraqis, Sudanese, Libyans; old men with henna-dyed beards from Baluchistan or the Frontier areas of Pakistan, Irani women clad in *chaddors*, men and women from the tropical areas of Africa with their distinctive dresses, and here and there such faces as can belong only to Europeans or Americans. It was this aspect of *hajj* which Malcolm-X commented on so eloquently in his *Autobiography*, describing it as a tremendously moving and almost unbelievable experience to be, for the first time in his life, regarded and respected simply as a human being who was the equal of every other human being without consideration of the usual man-made distinctions and barriers such as race, colour, nationality or social status. This is assuredly the ultimate experience in human Brotherhood known to man. And what is required of a pilgrim during *hajj* is not merely to be present, but to behave with kindness and consideration to one's fellow pilgrims (although in practice there are unfortunately many deviations from this requirement); indeed, one's entire pilgrimage can be rendered void by acts of harshness or hostility to others.

As we have seen, *hajj* takes place each year during the specified period of pilgrimage. However Muslims may visit the Ka'aba at any time to perform *'umrah,* the "Lesser Pilgrimage." The rites of *'umrah* consist simply of the assumption of *Ihram, tawaf* around the Ka'aba, and *sa'i.* Outside the season of *hajj,* countless Muslims visit Makkah to perform *'umrah* each year, and still others who live in Makkah or its vicinity visit the Sacred Mosque frequently for *salat,* meditation, reading the Qur'an, or to make *tawaf,* which in itself is a complete act of worship without performing *'umarh* or entering into the state of *Ihram.*

Although it is not in any way related to the observances of *hajj* or *'umarh*; those pilgrims who are able visit the city of Madinah some three hundred miles north of Makkah during their trip to Saudi Arabia. There they visit the grave of the Prophet (peace be on him), which is situated within the mosque which bears his name. The Prophet's Mosque stands at the site of the small mosque where he prayed and preached, next to which he had his home.

Visitors spend as much time as possible in the mosque engaged in *salat*, reading the Qur'an and meditation. The spirit of the Prophet seems to breathe within it, for it radiates an atmosphere of the deepest serenity and peace. As in Makkah, there are always visiting Muslims in Madinah, and it possesses the same unique flavour of peoples from all parts of the world coming together for the worship of Allah Most High—and here for the love and remembrance of His Holy Prophet (may Allah's peace and blessings be on him) as well.

SECTION TWO

Values and Morals

ISLAMIC VALUES AND QUALITIES:
THE ISLAMIC PERSONALITY

"Verily, men and women who submit, and men and women who believe, and men and women who are patient, and men and women who are truthful, and men and women who are humble before Allah, and men and women who give in Charity, and men and women who fast, and men and women who guard their chastity, and men and women who remember Allah much, to them Allah has promised forgiveness and a great reward." (33:35)

The goal of Islam—of its concepts, worships and teachings relating to values, attitudes, morals and behaviour—is to create an Islamic personality within the individual Muslim. Now just what is this "Islamic personality"?

Such a personality belongs to an individual who has rejected the supposition that there exists nothing but the material world, that the universe and one's own individual life, with all its circumstance and events, is the result of accident or blind chance, and who has accepted and lives by the certainty that there is a being who is responsible for all of creation and to Whom he, the human being, is in turn responsible. He acknowledges his dependence on this Being, accepts His laws as the rules which guide his life, and surrenders himself to Him. He is always conscious of Allah, remembering Him in all his activities and concerns. Islamic values and attitudes are the base on which his personality is built and Islamic criteria govern all aspects of his life.

Such an individual, together with others like himself, forms an Islamic society which, collectively, submits and conforms to the guidance of Almighty Allah. Islam proclaims that such Allah-conscious individuals, obedient to their Lord's commands, are the ones who will attain Allah's pleasure and His reward in the

Hereafter. A society composed of such individuals is therefore one which is capable of and suited to fulfilling the trust which Allah has bestowed on man of administering the earth and its affairs in a righteous and Allah-fearing manner.

We will now take a look at the attitudes and qualities which Islam enjoins and which it fosters in the true Muslim—qualities which can be found, even in today's disturbed world, turned as it is away from spiritual values and toward materialsim and the worship of self, in a striking manner in countless devout Muslims in all parts of the earth.

Allah-Consciousness *(Taqwa)*

"Verily, the Believers are those whose hearts feel fear when Allah is mentioned, and when His signs (or revelations) are recited to them they increase their faith, and who put their trust in their Lord." (8:2)

"Verily, those who live in awe for fear of their Lord, who believe in their Lord's signs (or revelations), who do not ascribe partners to their Lord, who give what they give in Charity with their hearts full of fear because they are to return to their Lord: it is these who hasten in all good acts and they are foremost in them." (23:57:61)

The Arabic word *taqwa*, denoting a quality which is absolutely essential in the personality of the conscious Muslim, has no exact English equivalent. *Taqwa* refers to an attitude comprised of love and fear of Allah which we may translate, for want of a better word, as "Allah-consciousness." More exactly, it refers to the constant awareness that one is always in front of Allah and that He knows everything concerning him, even his most secret thoughts. This attitude produces within one such an intense love for Allah that he wants to do only what is pleasing to Him; such great fear of Allah that he tries to avoid doing anything which He dislikes; and such a keen consciousness of Allah that he never for a single moment imagines His being unaware of what he does or that he will not be held accountable for all his intentions and actions. In the words of the Qur'an, the *muttaqeen* (those who possess *taqwa*) are:

> "Those who fear their Lord in their most secret thoughts
> and who hold the Hour (of Judgment) in awe." (21:49)

Taqwa is a vital attitude which develops little by little in the
heart of the Muslim child as he is taught about the existence and
omnipresence, the beneficence and kindness of Allah, his own
total dependence upon Him, his Sustainer, and his personal
responsibility and accountability to Him. Gradually there grows
within him a constant awareness of the fact that he is always
before Allah ("for," as the Prophet, peace be on him, said, "if you
do not see Him, He sees you"), a profound sense of personal
responsibility, the habit of judging all matters by Islamic rather
than by other criteria, and a love for Allah and for His way which
guides all his actions. This is supplemented and enhanced by
correct instruction in the principles and practices of Islam so that
it becomes his total frame of reference: by an awareness of social,
moral, political and other issues; and by the knowledge of the right
and wrong of things so that he can fulfill his responsibilities to
Allah, to other human beings and to society.

> "The *Muttaqeen* are those who spend (in Allah's way) in
> ease as well as in straitness, who restrain their anger and
> pardon men, for Allah loves those who do good; those
> who, when they commit an indecency or do injustice to
> their own souls, remember Allah and ask for forgiveness
> for their sins—and who can forgive sins except Allah?—
> and do not knowingly persist in what they have done. For
> these the reward will be forgiveness from their Lord and
> Gardens underneath which rivers flow, to abide therein,
> and (Allah's) favour, the reward of those who strive."
> (3:134-146)

Faith (*Iman*)

> "To Allah belong all things in the heavens and on earth,
> and Allah is sufficient as a protector." (4:132)

> "Say: 'He is my Lord; there is no deity except Him. In
> Him do I put my trust and to Him do I turn.'" (13:30)

Islam makes a distinction between a person who submits to
Allah's guidance by obeying His laws (a *muslim*) and one who has

the deep inner certainty of faith (a *mu'min:* one who possess iman), and indeed the difference is very significant. A *muslim* (submitter) may obey Allah's laws without real depth of faith, while a *mu'min* both possesses this faith and acts on it.

Now, faith to the *mu'min* is a great deal more than merely "believing" that Allah "exists." Such faith is rather the realization that this little piece of Reality which we are able to grasp with our minds or senses is only a minute portion of the greater Reality which is known only to its Creator. And it is the certainty that Allah is in absolute control of the universe, including man and his world, and that, together with the rest of Allah's creation, each one of us is wholly dependent upon Allah and will return to Him for accounting.

But let us go back to the beginning, starting from the most basic views of life in order to understand the meaning of such a faith more clearly. There can be only two possible logically—acceptable ways to explain the universe and all that takes place within it. Either it is, in totality, the result of randomness and chance interactions, the correct but completely accidental collusion of circumstances (which makes the earth nothing more than the accidentally "correct" combination of particles of matter and each new-born infant merely a fortuitously "right" organization of chromosomes, cellular structures, nerve connections and biochemical processes). In this case, the entire universe and all of human existence, including the events of each individual's life, can only be viewed as meaningless, purposeless accidentally-interacting phenomena, the result of blind chance in the grip of which a human being is simply a helpless, hopeless, struggling victim making motions which may or may not be of use. In the grip of such nothingness, he himself is a nothing, and his life has not the slightest sense or purpose: he simply is because he happens to have been born and has not yet died.

Such an explanation, which can produce nothing within the human soul except a despair too profound to be borne, is not only totally at variance with all the observed facts of the universe, which speak in endless volume of a planning, willing Power creative beyond human comprehension, negating randomness in their eloquent testimony to the incredible organizational Will behind all that exists;[1] it is also totally unacceptable to the human mind, itself an incredibly organized, purposeful entity which seeks meaning in everything. One who uses his reason therefore has no choice except to realize that all that exists must be the result of the will, the plan and the decision of a Supreme Power. And since this is so, likewise every circumstance and event, either within the physical world or within the world of man, must also fit in with the will, the plan, the decree of this Power. In short, nothing which either is or which takes place is outside Allah's plan and will and occurs only with His permission and decree, including the actions of men since man too is a part of the scheme of Allah's creation and a part of His plan. We will return to this point a little later.

It is easy enough to understand the meaningfulness and purposefulness of things in relation to phenomena or events which exhibit some logic, order or sense, some may say. But how are we to understand it in the face of natural disasters, unexpected catastrophes and human tragedies which seem to do violence to logic, to order, to meaning, crushing and destroying all that is good in human life?

Again, we return to the two possibilities: that everything is the result of randomness and chance, or that it is the result, although *why* may not always be apparent to our finite, limited human understanding, of Allah's all-wise plan. If the former is correct and we are dealing with random and consequently meaningless events, then logically *everything* must be accidental and meaningless, for it is not possible that part of existence is the result of a planning Will and has a meaning and purpose but some other part is accidental. Either all of it must be an accident, which it is impossible for the mind to accept, or all of it must be part of a plan

---

1. The Qur'an repeatedly appeals to human beings to use their reason to discover for themselves the undeniable evidences of this Power in the natural world, citing such examples as the alternation of night and day, the orbiting of the heavenly bodies, the earth and its geographic features, the multi-faceted uses of animals for men, man's own existence and his progress from state to state, the flight of birds, trees and fruits and crops, the oceans with their treasures and their utility to man, and many others.

and guided by the Planner. In either case the circumstances will of course be the same: whether we believe in the meaningfulness and purposefulness of all that takes place or we believe it to be the result of blind chance, we may equally in both instances from time to time find ourselves in the grip of events which we are utterly powerless to control. But the difference between these two views is nothing less than the difference between confidence and despair, between serenity of heart and endless, crushing anxiety: between living with trusting acceptance of what comes as being meaningful, purposeful and ultimately a source of good as it is the result of the will of the Merciful Allah, or with bitterness, anger, rebellion, and the intolerable weight of belief in nothingness.

At the same time, it is also clear that man has been endowed with freedom of choice and freedom to act. Does this not mean that he is, at least to some extent, independent and in charge of his own affairs? How does Islam resolve this very fundamental question of Allah's will in relation to man's freedom of choice and action?

To begin with, Islam places great emphasiz on action, repeatedly exhorting Muslims to strive, to make an effort, to do their best. Without action and effort nothing whatsoever can be attained or achieved. But at the same time, action and effort do not necessarily guarantee the results one desires.

Thus, for example, I make a decision, I choose a course of action, I act. To this extent I am free, within the range of choices available to me and depending on my capacity for action, which is obviously limited by my physical and mental condition and by the constraints of my environment. But what about the *outcome* of my decision, my choice, my action? Can I guarantee what it will be? No, I cannot. However, most of the time one's action *does* lead to the desired results. For example, I decide to get up out of my chair and I am able to do it; I decide to go to work in my car and I go; I decide to get married, or to get a new job, or to invent a nuclear submarine or a Boeing 747 or to go to the moon, and I do all these things, dependent only on myself, on the cooperation of my fellow human beings, and on various machines and inventions. How then can one assert that I am not in control and that I do not determine the outcome of my actions? In short, where does Allah come into the picture?

Let us examine the matter in greater depth. It is obvious that to achieve the results I want I must will and act. I can hardly expect to get to work if I spend the morning lying in bed, to get a new job if I don't go out and look for one, or to get to the moon without the necessary efforts on my part to master the essential knowledge and skills. But even then my efforts do not guarantee the results I seek. All that may be said is that, although the degree of effort has a direct relationship to the probability of achieving a desired outcome, nevertheless the outcome may turn out to be quite different than one intends. For example, I decide to get out of my chair as I've done thousands of times in the past but instead of doing it I collapse with a heart attack. I leave my house to go to work, having no doubt that I'll get there as I've done day after day for many years but I have an accident on the way and never arrive. I'm rich, famous and beloved but one day I learn that I have a fatal illness and in spite of all the medical skills money can provide I die in the prime of my youth and career. I'm about to be launched in a spacecraft similar to others which have carried out their missions brilliantly but something goes wrong and it burns up in the take-off—one could go on and on enumerating examples.

In earlier times when life was simpler, few people entertained any question about the existence of Allah and His controlling will. They knew that their lives were dependent upon crops which were dependent upon such factors as rainfall and sunshine, which depended immediately upon what Allah willed. They knew, too, the limitations of their capacities to act, to shape their destinies, and these, too, were referred back to Allah's decision. But today, when our lives are run to such a large extent by the products of science and technology, we depend upon these—as if they were gods themselves—for the very control of our existence. We have totally lost sight of the fact that while we have been given the power—and indeed the obligation—to think, to plan, to choose and to act, we do not necessarily determine the outcome of our actions which depends upon what Allah wills. Nor do our existence, our faculties, our powers and capacities to act depend upon ourselves. Does any of us make ourselves so that we can determine our appearance or size or shape, our colour or physical condition, our intellectual endowments and talents? And is there a single one of us who can by our own efforts control the beating of our hearts, the working of the cells and tissues in our bodies, the eventual process of disintegration and decline of old age, an accident or illness which overtakes us, or the death which is our inevitable destiny? If not, then the assertion that we are in control of our lives and are self-sufficient, which is the proud boast of contemporary Western civilization, is merely wishful thinking and self-delusion.

This notion of man's self-sufficiency has unfortunately led Western man to the conclusion that because he is able to do most of what he wills and undertakes, it is solely his willing and doing, aided by the invention and utilisation of high-powered technological devices, which determines the results he achieves. Both man and his inventions are presumed independent of anything except each other, and the fact that there must be Someone who gives man his nature and the capacity, power and means to carry out what he undertakes, and Who at the same time determines the results of his undertakings, has been totally lost sight of. Consequently, although many people still profess belief in Him, Allah, as the sustaining, planning, willing, acting Power in the universe, has been largely discounted in explaining the phenomena of "Nature," as well as in relation to human affairs, and hence He has been "retired" from the lives of so many of us. In passage after passage, the Qur'an addresses itself to this point:

> "It is He Who created for you ears and eyes and hearts. Little do you give thanks! And it is He Who spread you in the earth, and unto Him will you be gathered. And it is He Who gives life and death, and His is the alternation of night and day. Do you then have no intelligence? Nay, but they say the like of what was said by earlier peoples. They say: 'When we are dead and have become dust and bones, shall we then really be raised again? We were already promised this, we and our, forefathers. Truly, this is nothing except tales of the ancients.' Say: 'Unto Whom belongs the earth and whatsoever is in it, if you have knowledge?' They will say: 'To Allah.' Say: 'Will you not then remember? Say: 'Who is Lord of the seven heavens and Lord of the exalted throne (of authority)?' They will say: '(They belong) to Allah.' Say: 'Will you not then be dutiful to Him?' Say: 'In whose hand is the dominion over

ail things, and He protects while there is no protection against Him, if you have knowledge?' They will say: '(It belongs)' to Allah. 'Say: 'Then how are you deluded?' "

(23:78-89)

And again:

"And among His signs is that He created you from dust, and then, behold, you are human beings scattered (far and wide). And among His signs is that He created for you mates from among yourselves, that you may dwell with them in tranquillity, and He has put love and mercy between your (hearts). Verily in that are signs for those who reflect. And among His Signs is the creation of the heavens and the earth, and the variations of your languages and your colours. Verily in that are signs for those who know. And among His signs is the sleep you take by night and by day, and your quest (for a livelihood) from His bounty. In that are signs for those who hearken. And among His signs He shows you the lightning in fear and hope, and He spends down rain from the sky and with it gives life to the earth after it is dead. Verily in that are signs for those who are wise. And among His signs is that the heavens and the earth stand by His command. Then when He calls you with a call, behold, from the earth you will come froth. To Him belongs every being in the heavens and the earth: all are obedient to Him. It is He Who begins creation, then repeats it, and this is easy for Him. To Him pertain the loftiest similitudes in the heavens and the earth, for He is the Exalted, the Wise." (30:20-27)

And yet again:

"All that is in the heavens and all that is in the earth glorifies Allah. Unto Him belongs the dominion and unto Him belongs the praise, and He has power over all things. It is He Who created you, yet one of you is a disbeliever and one of you is a believer, and Allah sees all that you do. He created the heavens and the earth in truth, and He shaped you and made you with good shapes, and unto Him is the journeying. He knows all that is in the heavens and the earth, and He knows all that you conceal and all that you reveal. And Allah is the Knower of what is in the hearts (of human beings)."   (64:1-4)

"And with Him are the keys of the Unseen; none knows
them but He, And He knows whatever is in the land and
the sea. Not a leaf falls but He knows it, nor a seed grain
grows in the darkness of the earth, nor anything fresh or
dry but is (inscribed) in a clear Book. And it is He Who
takes your souls by night and Who knows what you have
done by day; then He revives you by day that a term
appointed may be fulfilled. Then to Him will be your
return, and then will He declare to you all that you did."

(6:59-60)

"Say: 'Shall I take for my protector any other than Allah,
the Maker of the heavens and the earth? And it is He that
feedeth (His creatures) but is not fed.... If Allah touch thee
with affliction, none can remove it but He; and if He touch
thee with good, (know that) He has power over everything.
He is the irresistible, (high) above His slaves: and He is
the Wise, the Informed'.... Say: Do you think that if
Allah's punishment were to come upon you, or the Last
Hour, you would then call upon something other than
Allah (Answer) if you are among the truthful! Nay, you
would call upon Him, and if He willed, He would remove
what occasioned your call upon Him, and you would
forget those whom you had set up as partners with Him'
.... Say: 'Do you think that if Allah took away your
hearing and your sight and set a seal upon your hearts,
there is a deity besides Allah who could restore them to
you?'"

Say: 'Who is it that delivers you from perils in the
darkness of the land or sea, upon Whom you call humbly
and in secret: "If He only delivers us from this (affliction),
we will be among the grateful"? 'Say: 'It is Allah Who
delivers you from these and from all (other) distresses and
yet you associate others with Him.'"

(6:14, 17-18, 40-41, 46, 63-64)

For indeed, when any of us is in a state of danger, terror or
crisis, it is not other people or technology we call on; almost
instinctively, as a matter of course, we call upon Allah, even if we
otherwise never think of Him or even deny His existence. Anyone
who has ever been in a battle or a wreck at sea or a devastating
flood or earthquake or tornado (an "act of Allah"), or in the grip

of a terrible illness or personal tragedy knows this and many have become believer as a result of such experience. For at such a time each one of us recognizes the utter powerlessness of human beings and their inventions. We know unquestioningly that nothing can help or save us except the Supreme Power of the heavens and the earth, and quite unconsciously and without concern for our previous beliefs in the matter, we instinctively cry to Him for aid. And what about at the time of death? Is there a single one of us who then still entertains the illusion that man is in control and has anything to say about his own destiny, or who calls upon anyone or anything except Allah. For that is the supreme moment of truth, the truth which has always been there before our eyes but from which many of us turned away, as if deaf and blind, time and time again during the span of our lives.

In Islam we find the correct perspective concerning man's freedom of choice and action and the limits of his capacity to control events. For Islam informs us that every single thing in the universe, every atom of creation, is always dependent on Allah not only for its very being but for its continuance and functioning as well. In this human beings are no different from the rest of creation; despite the illusion that we are in control, our being is dependent on Him and we are sustained by Him at every moment of our lives, whether we are peacefully relaxing in the security and comfort of our homes or are in a state of critical danger or affliction.

This state of dependency, helplessness and creatureliness in relation to Allah is expressed in Arabic by the single concise word *'ubudiyat,* that is, the condition of being Allah's *'abd,* the nearest English equivalent for which is "slave": one with whom Allah does as He pleases because he belongs on Him, who is totally at His disposal and in a state of utter dependence and humility before Him. To the devout Muslim, the highest honour and the fulfillment of his existence lies in being the *'abd* of Allah Most High,[2] and of

---

2. *Abd-Allah*, the meaning of the Arabic name 'Abdullah. See Footnote 1, page 50 for an elaboration of the significance of the concept of man's *'ubudiyat* to Allah in relation to the Holy Prophet's being, no less than any other human being of any status, Allah's humble slave.

no one and nothing except Him. And part of the condition of this *'ubudiyat* consists of the realization that man's task is to choose, to will, to act and to strive his utmost but that it is Allah Who determines the results of this striving as He sees fit. Therefore, beyond his capacity to act and to shape events by his action, the *mu'min* (sincere believer) trusts in and depends on Allah completely for the outcome of his affairs, assured that nothing that happens to him or to any other creature is a random, chance event, an "accident" or "coincidence," but has a meaning and a purpose which are known to Allah.

But we must be careful not to misunderstand this point, as many people have done and sooner or later lost their "faith" as a result. It certainly does not mean that if a person trusts in and depends on Allah in all his affairs, Allah will in return keep all trouble and suffering away from him; in other words, "If I'm good Allah won't let anything bad happen to me." Indeed, this is not the way Allah has ordained this life, nor is this the attitude of a true believer. Allah sends both ease and suffering to all, the wicked and saintly alike, and certainly the sincere believer, like every other descendant of Adam, has his share of troubles, illnesses and Calamities; in truth, he is more likely to pass through suffering and adversity as a result of his unswerving commitment to the right and his consequent lack of concern for personal comfort and worldly advantage. The difference is not in the circumstances but in the attitude; for the believer possesses the absolute certainty that Allah is in complete control of everything, knowing what man with his finite. limited human understanding cannot know, and since he believes that whatever Allah sees fit to send has a meaning and a purpose, he accepts it with the hope and assurance that it may hold some good for him either in this world or in the Hereafter.

For the whole of this life, both the good and the bad of it, constitutes a trial and a test for the human individual by means of which his quality and his state in the future existence are determined. Again and again the Qur'an speaks of this:

> "Every soul must taste death; and We test you by evil and by good by way of trial. And unto Us will you return."
>
> (21:35)

> "Do men think that they will be left alone on saying, 'We believe', and that they will not be tested? And assuredly We tested those before them. Thus Allah knows those who are sincere and knows those who are pretenders."
>
> (29:2-3)

But the test does not lie only in hardship and suffering. The rich, powerful and healthy individual is tested just as much by his wealth, rank and good physical condition as is the poor one by his poverty or the sick or handicapped by his affliction; indeed, the one to whom more has been given in the way of health or possession or talents or status or power will be held accountable for more. What is of ultimate importance is not how much or little one possesses of all these benefits but what he does with whatever he has been given. For although a human being may not necessarily have a great deal to say concerning the conditions of his life or the outcome of a specific situation, nevertheless he is accountable both for his actions and for his inner response to the particular conditions in which he found himself. The notion that a person's spirit and his deeds cannot rise above difficult or disadvantaged circumstances is one which Islam rejects, just as it rejects mechanistic views of any aspect of life. Man is not a robot. Even in the worst of circumstances human beings have kept alive the spark of humanity and decency in their breasts and acted in ways which would do credit to the Angels.

Therefore, when faced with difficulties, the *mu'min* does all he can to deal with or to remove them, for he is not supposed to allow himself to be distressed or to bear suffering unnecessarily, and is expected to strive with all his strength to improve his situation. But if the desired results are not attained in spite of all his efforts, he does not despair nor does he dictate terms to Allah but rather tries to be patient and steadfast with what the Qur'an calls a "beautiful patience" (70:5). The Qur'an speaks in moving language of the way in which a sincere believer should bear trouble and affliction:

> "And We shall undoubtedly test you with something of fear and hunger, some loss of wealth and lives and fruits. But give glad tidings to the patient, who say, when afflicted with calamity, 'To Allah we belong and to Him

is our return'.[3] They are, those upon whom is Allah's blessing and mercy, and they are the ones who are guided."
(2:155.157)

"They who are patient, seeking the pleasure of their Lord, who are regular in *salat*, who spend (in Charity) secretly and openly out of what Allah has bestowed on them, and who repel evil with good: for them is the attainment of the Final Abode."   (13:22)

"... And give thou good tidings to the humble, whose hearts tremble when Allah is mentioned and who are patient under that which afflicts them, and who are constant in *salat* and who spend (in Charity) out of what We bestow on them."   (22:34.35)

Indeed, as a rule the *mu'min* does not ask Allah for the specific outcome of a situation, for he realises that he cannot know with certainty what is best for him even in relation to this life, much less in relation to the Hereafter. Rather he asks Allah to guide him and make easy for him what is for his good in this world and in the future Life, and to keep him away from whatever is bad or harmful to him in either. For the *mu'min*, not knowing positively himself wherein his good lies, possesses the assurance that Allah, Who does know, is able to send good to him even through the greatest suffering and trial. Moreover, he has the deep certainty that any trouble, pain or affliction which he experiences—even, as the Prophet (peace be on him) said, to the pricking of the foot of the believer by a thron—is an expiation for sins, a source of reward in the Hereafter if it is borne with patience and endurance, and a means of coming nearer to Allah Most High through that ineffable softening of the heart which suffering brings through complete trust and reliance upon Him. In such a situation the *mu'min* finds the greatest solace and comfort of heart in the remembrance of Allah Most High, holding fast to Him, depending completely upon Him, and contemplating His beneficence and exalted glory with words of praise and adoration in the total surrender of his will and his being to what He, the Praised and Exalted, sees fit to send. The Qur'an speaks of

---

3. These are the words with which a *mu'min* receives the news of a death or any calamity.

"Those who believe and whose hearts find comfort in the
remembrance of Allah. Lo! in the remembrance of Allah
do hearts find comfort."   (13:28)

Thus even trouble and distress constitute great sources of good
to the one whose heart is firmly fixed upon his Lord and contented
with His decree, and such people are often able to remain
uncomplaining, thankful and to experience deep peace of heart
even in the mindst of the greatest trials.

Then what does such a person feel about death, either of
himself or of a near one? To the *mu'min* death is simply the return
of the soul to Him Who gave it, the last stage of the journey "from
Allah to Allah": as such, it holds no terrors for him except the fear
that he may not have deserved the pleasure of his Lord, Whose
love he desires, Whose anger he dreads, and Whose mercy he
hopes for with all his being. The inevitability of death and the
Hereafter is never far from his consciousness, serving to keep all
his life and deeds in perspective as he tries at all times to live in
preparedness for what is to come and to send ahead for his soul
such deeds as will make heavy his balance of good when he
appears before his Lord. And when death claims someone near to
him, he does not indulge in excesses of grief (for not only does
Islam forbid this but its in appropriateness in one who believes is
obvious) but prays for Allah's mercy and peace on the departed,
and takes his living and dying as a lesson and example.

Islam very strongly emphasizes the distinction between a believer
and a nonbeliever, both in terms of their inner state and their true
worth. The reason for this may now be apparent. A person devoid
of belief and faith and a believer alike are both equally helpless
and dependent on the Almighty Power in the universe, of course,
but the nonbeliever is either unaware of this or denies, rejects and
resents the fact of his *'ubudiyat* vis-a-vis Allah. As he does not
acknowledge the existence of a Reality other than that which he
can perceive or comprehend, insisting on the supremacy of the
material world and ascribing to it ultimate value and importance,
he does not acknowledge any authority over his life except that of
his own desires or the dictates of other human beings or "society."
Such an individual totally lacks accuracy of perspective concerning

himself and his life in this world. He is in a state of forgetfulness
and heedlessness concerning essential matters, while he preoccupies
and busies himself with what is trivial. He is like one rushing
blindly, pell-mell, in his intense involvement with the world—with
material things, activities or pleasures, no matter how shallow and
meaningless—often in a desperate effort to avoid having to come
to grips with the emptiness, restlessness and dissatisfaction inside
him which is the natural consequence of his deep alienation from
his Creator, himself and the universe he lives in. And yet such
individual usually imagines that he is "free" and not the slave of
anyone or anything!

If we could look into the heart of the *mu'min* by way of
comparison, we would find an individual at peace and in harmony
with his place in the universe, submitting to what Allah ordains for
him and to His guidance willingly, gladly and with awe and fear
of his Lord. We would find one who feels at home with all of
Allah's creation because he knows his rightful place in it and
hence does not fight with it or try to exploit or harm it. We would
find a person who, in times of trouble, resists disturbing his soul
by asking "Why?" or imagining all he "might have done" to avert
it, for he possesses the deep certainty that every circumstance and
happening in his life is the result of Allah's all-wise decree,
coming to him as ordained no matter what anyone might or might
not do, and that what is required of him in response is patience,
steadfastness and complete trust in Allah. Conversely, if good
comes to him, he responds by a profound sense of humility and
thankfulness to Allah from whom it came rather than with pride
and preoccupation with his own powers or merits. He maintains a
constant perspective within himself: the awareness of the transitory
and finite nature of this brief life in comparison with the enduring
life of the Hereafter, and the desire, which is greater than any
other, to attain the good of that Life by every means in his power.

Such an individual, by means of this perspective, never loses
sight of where he is going or his ultimate goal: to merit Allah's
mercy and pleasure, and thereby to attain the Eternal Home. As
part of the means of attaining it, he is active in the world, taking
his responsibilities seriously and trying to fulfill them to the best

of his abilities, and being always conscious of his duty to society. But he is not in love with this world and avoids becoming entangled with material preoccupations because there are more important concerns at the centre of his life. His constant prayer is, "Our Lord, give us good in this world and good in the Hereafter, and save us from the punishment of the Fire." To him faith is life itself, without which he could not continue the struggle of existence for one single minute.

> "Verily. this world's life is transient, but the Hereafter is
> the Permanent Abode."   (40:39)

Taqwa and *iman* are the two most basic and essential qualities of the *muslim* and the *mu'min*. We will now continue our survey of the qualities and characteriztics which Islam enjoins and which it considers essential in an Islamic personality.

Sincerity

Without this quality the Muslim's relationship with both Allah and his fellow men is null and void. Sincerity toward Allah should prompt him to wholeheartedness in worship, to absolute honesty with himself regarding his motives and intentions, and to striving continually to weed out of his character whatever has a trace of hypocrisy, greed, selfishness, envy or the desire for reputation or power, while sincerity toward his fellow human beings should lead him to behave in an open and straight-forward manner with them. He should not use or manipulate them for his own purposes, and should genuinely desire their good, liking for them what he likes for himself. He should say what he means, refrain from saying what he does not mean, and should say whatever needs to be said to the other's face rather than behind his back. His relations with others are not to be superficial, casual or careless, and he is expected to interact with everyone responsibly, sincerely and in a meaningful fashion.

Responsibility

This is the keynote of the Muslim's behaviour-toward Allah, toward other human beings, and toward the rest of His creation, both animate and inanimate. His task is first to fulfill his own obligations to Allah and to other people, regardless of what others may do, and then to try to change, as far as is in his power, whatever he sees that is wrong and evil. His attitude should never be, "Am I my brother's keeper?" But, "I am responsible for doing whatever I can," for he knows that he will be held accountable not only for his own attitudes and actions but for anything else over which he had control or influence in the society and the world around him as well.

Integrity

Because the Muslim has an ever-present consciousness of Allah and his responsibility to Him, every aspect and act of his life is to be constantly submitted to the standards and criteria of Islam. Nothing is outside the pale of it, from the most private and personal matters to the most public. The standards of Islam are supposed to be so much a part of his very nature that it is difficult for him to knowingly disregard and disobey them in any aspect. And if he does so, his inner attunement to himself and to Allah's guidance should be so keen that he is at once aware of his mistake and asks for Allah's forgiveness.

Honesty, Truthfulness, Keeping of Commitments, Fair-Dealing

Since obedience to such principles is basic to mutual trust, responsibility and reliability among human beings as well as to integrity within the personality, these are among the most emphasized qualities in Islam. Such a scrupulous adherence to truth includes absolute honesty and fidelity in all personal relationships and interactions, in business dealings and transactions, and in the administration of justice. The Qur'an enjoins these qualities over and over again:

> "O you who believe, be conscious of Allah and be with the truthful."   (9:119)

> "(The virtuous are) those who honour their trusts and promises and those who stand firm in their testimonies..."
> (70:32-33)

> "O you who believe, stand out firmly for justice, bearers of witness for Allah, even though it be against yourselves

or your parents or near relatives. Whether he is rich or
poor, Allah's claim takes precedence over (the claims of)
either of them. So do not follow your own desires lest you
swerve from justice; and if you lapse or fall away (from
truth), then verily, Allah is aware of what you do."

(4:135)

"... And keep (your) commitments: verily, concerning
commitments (you) will be questioned. Fill the measure
when you measure, and weigh with a right balance; that
is good and right in the end."   (17:34-35)

And among many *Hadiths* concerning these virtues, the following:

"There are three characteriztics of a hypocrite: when he
speaks he lies, when he makes a promise he acts
treacherously against it, and when he is trusted he betrays."

makes it very clear how essential such qualities are in the personality
of the Muslim.

Discipline and Self-Control

As we have seen, to live the life of a Muslim with its five daily
prayers, month of fasting each year, and obedience to all the
injunctions of Islam, a considerable degree of self-discipline is
needed. This discipline is fostered by the Muslim's continual
awareness that he is not his own master but rather Allah's slave,
who stands ever ready to bear and to obey his Lord's commands.

Self-control in governing one's temper is very strongly stressed,
and forbearance and making allowances for others' faults are
enjoined. In the case of a personal injury, the Muslim is urged to
forgive and, although retaliation is permitted, to forgo it for the
sake of Allah out of mercy and compassion to the one who has
wronged him. While Islam discourages asceticism and permits the
enjoyment of Allah's bounties, the Muslim is expected to keep his
appetites and desires under control rather than allowing them to
control him. Self-discipline and self-control are reflected in many
aspects of both the private and the public life of Muslims, from the
degree of self-control shown by a Muslim to whom wrong has been
done but who keeps his tongue and hand (and with them his heart)

from vengefulness, to the orderly and correct manner in which Muslims line themselves up for a congregational prayer.

Humility, Patience, Endurance, Courage, Thankfulness

The true Muslim is under no illusions about his own greatness or importance; he is humble about his attainments and aware of his own limitations. He does not seek fame or power but rather the pleasure and approval of Allah, trying to be useful in whatever way he can. As we have seen, he tries to endure unavoidable trouble and suffering patiently and courageously, finding solace and comfort in the remembrance of Allah, and he is thankful for all good that comes his way. Phrases expressing his dependence on and praise of Allah form a vital part of his speech patterns.[4] He does not despair in any situation, knowing that everything is possible for Allah. In any case, the events of this life are not the most important thing to him, but rather to attain Allah's pleasure and His mercy in the Life-to-Come.

Dignity, Honour and Self-Respect

A strong sense of honour and self-respect is an essential quality in the true Muslim. Even the most humble—an illiterate peasant or labourer—often demonstrates a striking degree of uprightness and dignity.

The Muslim's dignity stems from his being the slave of and fearing no one except his Creator; no one can threaten or intimidate him for he knows that what befalls him depends not on other people but on the Lord of the people. Thus he maintains his dignity and serenity even though his life may be full of hardships. His self-respect is the product of the innate straightness of his world-view, concepts and characters, and he tries never to do anything which will lower him in his own estimation or that of others—and above all in his Lord's. He realises that the only real distinction he or any other human being can achieve is due to his degree of *taqwa, iman*

---

4. For example. *"Insha'Allah"* (if Allah wills). *"Ma'sha'Allah"* (as Allah has willed it). *"SubhanAllah"* (glory be to Allah!). *"Alhamdulillah"* (praise be to Allah). *"Astagh firAllah"* (may Allah forgive). *"JazakAllah al-khair"* (may Allah reward you with good), and many others.

and knowledge rather than race, wealth, social status and the like. And as he has his honour, he recognizes and upholds the right of others to theirs, and tries to refrain from behaviour which would violate it such as gossiping, prying into people's affairs, being suspicious or interfering with other's privacy.

Purity, Modesty and Chastity

To the true Muslim, man and woman alike, anything impure or degrading is abhorrent and to be avoided at all costs. Sexual purity thus begins in the mind of the believer with the fear of Allah and the desire to maintain that state of inner balance and cleanness which is essential to his or her integrity and well-being. Strict modesty of dress, manner and behaviour, and absolute chastity both before and after marriage are required.

Kindness, Helpfulness, Cooperation

Islam teaches that human beings are all equally creatures of Allah, all sharing the same condition. The Muslim's obligation is to live in cooperation, not competition, with his fellow men and to be helpful, kind, just and compassionate toward everyone, regardless of whether they are of the same or a different faith, race, culture or status, etc. Kindness to animals as well as to human beings is required, for abuse or cruelty of any of Allah's creatures is abhorrent to their Creator. Such virtues are stressed again and again in the Qur'an and in the Prophet's *Hadiths*, as for example the following:

> "Allah will not show mercy to him who does not show mercy to others." *(Hadith)*

> The Prophet (peace be on him) said, "I swear by Allah he does not believe. I swear by Allah he does not believe. I swear by Allah he does not believe." He was asked who it was and replied, "The one from whose injurious conduct his neighbour is not safe." *(Hadith)*

> "The Believer is not one who eats his fill when his neighbour beside him is hungry." *(Hadith)*

> "All creatures are Allah's children, and those dearest to Allah are the ones who treat His children kindly." *(Hadith)*

Charitableness, Generosity and Hospitality

Our brief discussion of *zakat* has already given some idea of how much Islam stresses charitableness and generosity. Indeed, the emphasiz is so great that Charity is enjoined in verse after verse of the Qur'an often together with the obligation of *salat*. Numerous occasions have been specified for the giving of Charity, for example, on the two 'Eids or festivals; as an expiation if one is unable to fast during Ramadan due to pregnancy, suckling an infant, a permanent illness, or old age; during Ramadan by those who are fasting; by remitting a debt to a debtor; or by the ransoming or freeing of captives, etc. This repeated and continuous emphasiz on Charity in Islam does not allow the Muslim to forget the needs of his brothers and sisters who are less fortunate but to feel them as his own.

But in Islam Charity does not consist merely of help to the needy; rather it includes anything one does which is of good to others. A *Hadith* of the Prophet (peace be on him) mentions that Charity includes removing thorns from the road and smiling at one's brother. And open-handedness in spending and giving are to be practiced not only toward the poor but also toward one's family, relatives, friends, neighbours, guests, and even strangers. The good things the Muslim has are to be shared, not kept solely for himself. Generosity and hospitality are thus highly-valued qualities among Muslims in every part of the world.

Consideration and Good Manners

Prophet Muhammad (peace be on him) was a living example of the finest and most beautiful manners, and he stressed politeness and consideration as an expression of the Muslim's faith. Basically this means to treat other human beings as they like to be treated and as one like to be treated oneself, whether they are Muslims or non-Muslims, relatives, friends, strangers, and even one's enemies.

Brotherliness

In innumerable Qur'anic verses and *Hadiths* of the Prophet (peace be on him) we find delineated the nature of the relationship which should exist among Muslims. One's fellow-Muslims are other "selves" for whom the Muslim should desire what he desires for himself and dislike what he dislikes for himself, rejoicing at· their good fortune and sharing in their griefs. The following are a few well-known *Hadiths* which convey so expressively the sense of love and brotherliness which Muslims should feel for one another. The Holy Prophet (peace be on him) said:

> "By Him in Whose hand is my soul, a man does not believe until he loves for his brother what he loves for himself." *(Hadith)*

> "Your see the Believers in their mutual pity, love and affection like one body. When one member has a complaint, the rest of the body is united with it in wakefulness and fever." *(Hadith)*

> "A Muslim is a Muslim's brother; he does not wrong him or abandon him. If anyone cares for his brother's need Allah will care for his need; if anyone removes his brother's anxiety Allah will remove from him one of the anxieties on the Day of Resurrection; and if anyone conceals a Muslim's secrets Allah will conceal his secrets on the Day of Resurrection." *(Hadith)*

Observing the interaction among conscientious Muslims, others are often impressed by their warm brotherly or sisterly behaviour toward each other, and by the sincerity, openness, kindness and meaningfulness which characterizes their relationships, particularly in contrast to the shallowness and meaninglessness of so much of present-day interaction among human beings.

Warmth and Lovingness

Although Muslims may be reserved in public, with intimates they are as a rule very warm human beings. This capacity for warmth and affection stems from the love and security which is received in childhood through close relationships with parents and other family members. This is expressed in cheerfulness, good-temper, a sense of humour, loyalty in relationships, very warm ties with family and friends, love for children, and consideration for other people and their feelings.

Striving and Hard Work

The Qur'an states that "Man shall have nothing but what he strives for" (53:39) and there are numerous *Hadiths* enjoining and encouraging working and striving in the worldly realm. Muslims are expected to develop their skills and talents, and to utilise and manage the earth's resources; however, this is to be done in a manner which is for the benefit of society and in keeping with the Islamic goals and values. It is also a fundamental responsibility of Muslims to try to shape the conditions of society and the world for good, and to contribute their utmost to the welfare of their communities.

Love of Knowledge

The Prophet (peace be on him) proclaimed that seeking knowledge is a duty on every Muslim man and woman, and indeed the love of knowledge has been a characteriztic of Muslims from the earliest times. As a result, as history attests, at a time when Europe was still extremely primitive and undeveloped, Muslims possessed highly-developed science, mathematics, medicine and literature. Knowledge and understanding are among the most important characteriztics of a true Muslim, for without them his Islam is likely to be mere imitation and he will lack the ability to manage the affairs of his society and the world, or even of his own family, in a correct and appropriate manner.

ISLAMIC MORALS AND BEHAVIOUR

"The (true) slaves of the Merciful are those who walk on the earth in humility, and when the ignorant address them, they say, 'Peace'; those who pass the night prostrating themselves and standing before their Lord, and those who say 'Our Lord, avert from us the torment of Hell; indeed, the torment of it is anguish and indeed, it is evil as an abode and station.' And those who, when they spend, are neither extravagant nor miserly; for between them (these extremes) is a just course. And those who do not call upon any other deity with Allah, and do not take a life which Allah has made sacred except in the way of justice, nor commit adultery—and whoever does this will pay the penalty.... And those who do not witness falsehood, and when they pass by what is vain pass by with honour; and those who, when they are reminded of the revelations of their Lord, do not fall down deaf and blind thereat; and who say, `Our Lord, grant us comfort in our spouses and our offspring, and make us examples for those who are Allah-conscious.' They will be awarded a place in Heaven because they were patient, and they will meet therein with welcome and peace, abiding there (forever). Beautiful is it as an abode and station!" (25:63.68, 72-76)

It cannot be stressed strongly enough that Islam is not a mere belief system nor a "religion" in the commonly-understood sense of the word. Rather it is what in Arabic is called a *deen*: a total frame of reference, a complete system and way of life which embraces the entirety of man's existence. It does not separate what pertains to "religion," such as acts of worship, from what pertains to human interaction and mundane or "secular" life. Consequently there is no fragmentation or division within the personality of the Muslim due to the splitting of life into compartments or applying different rules or criteria to different parts of life. The same Divine system, the same Allah-given laws and standards govern all aspects of life, and all of an individual's actions are considered by Islam as worship in the broad sense of the term if they are done with the sincere intention of pleasing Allah in keeping with His injunctions.

Neither is Islam a vague, amorphous religion which is satisfied with merely asking people to be kind, good and morally upright. It is clear and specific about matters which are prohibited (*haram*), as well as about those which are obligatory (*fard*), and about these there is no question. Among permissible (*halal*) things there are degrees, with classifications such as "meritorious," "detestable" or "neutral." The guide for the Muslim's conduct in all spheres of his life is, first, the Holy Qur'an and, second, the Prophet's example or practice (the *Sunnah*, which relates to what he himself did, recommended or approved of in others, and the *Hadith*, which relates to what he said). Hence the Muslim does not have to grope

about or to wonder if a given behaviour is good or bad. If it is bad
it will be prohibited by a clear text either in the Qur'an or the
Hadith; otherwise, in general, if no text exists in either of these
prohibiting it, it is not because Allah forgot but because He did not
intend to prohibit it because in His knowledge it is not harmful.

Although this is a very complex subject which is beyond the
scope of this book, it is important to mention that besides being the
guide for the individual Muslim's conduct, the Qur'an and the
Sunnah also constitute the sources of Islamic legislation known as
the *Shar'iah*. From this vast body of principles has been derived
a system of Islamic jurisprudence known as *Fiqh* which deals with
all aspects of life, both individual and collective. The Hanafi,
Hanbali, Maliki, Shafi'i and Ja'fari *madhabs* are actually various
schools of Islamic jurisprudence, not separate sects within Islam,
as many people erroneously believe.[1]

The principles governing morals and behaviour in Islam can be
stated as follows. First, everything is permissible except what the
Law-Giver, Allah Himself, has clearly prohibited either in Qur'an
or through the Prophet's *Sunnah*, which is a practical interpretation
of the Qur'an. No human being can claim or is entitled to the
authority to make something permissible or prohibited, for this
authority belongs to Allah alone. Accordingly, attempting to make
something prohibited which is permissible, and vice-versa, is
tantamount to *shirk*, that is, ascribing divinity to something other
than Allah because the authority and the right to legislate morals
and behaviour belongs to Allah alone.

---

1. A word needs to be said here about the terms Sunni and Shi'ah. These
    denote groupings within the community of Islam based not on differences
    in fundamentals of belief but rather on the concept of successorship to
    the Prophet (peace be on him). Sunnis hold that the Prophet did not
    designate anyone to succeed him as the leader and head of the Muslim
    ummah and state after his death, and thus the first four caliphs were
    rightfully chosen from among the people, while Shi'ahs hold that the
    Prophet designated 'Ali, his cousin and son-in-law, as his successor,
    and that the leader of the *ummah* should be from among the Pophet's
    descendants through 'Ali and his wife Fatimah, the daughter of the
    Prophet. Although the difference of view-point between Shi'ahs and
    Sunnis have been widely publicised, within the mainstream of Shi'ah
    thought they do not conern basic conceptions, teachings or practices
    and are on the whole relatively minor in nature.

Another principle of Islamic law is that whatever leads to prohibited things is itself prohibited. Moreover, what is doubtful or equivocal should be avoided lest it eventually involve one in what is unlawful, and one should not place himself in situations of temptation or approach near to what is prohibited. Playing with Allah's injunctions and resorting to trickery or deceit to make the unlawful seem permissible is also obviously prohibited. Good intentions are not an excuse for doing what is unlawful; a good end does not justify a wrong means in Islam. And what is unlawful is unlawful for everyone without regard to sex, status, wealth or any other criterion whatsoever, for in Islam things are not forbidden to the ordinary citizen but allowed to "special" people, or permitted to men but forbidden to women; the head of state, the most eminent religious scholar and the lowliest beggar, and every man as well as every woman, alike are subject to the same laws. Finally, unlawful things may be treated as lawful for a very temporary period and subject to extremely strict rules in the case of very urgent, compelling necessity. For example, although the eating of pork is strictly prohibited, if one is without food of any kind to the point of starvation, he may resort to the consumption of pork, but only in that minimal amount which meets his bare needs and without any greed or desire for the prohibited thing.

The laws given by Allah for man's guidance are moral and spiritual principles just as vital and binding as the natural laws which He has ordained for the physical universe, and just as certain in their operation. And Allah's laws, whether for man or for the rest of the natural world, are never whimsical or arbitrary but rather the result of His infinite knowledge of what is for the good of His creatures. Indeed, He has prohibited only those things which are injurious or undesirable for human beings. Thus the fundamental principle governing Islamic morals and behaviour is that whatever is beneficial is permitted and whatever is harmful to man—that is, whatever degrades him, lowers his dignity as a human being, hurts his body, mind or soul, or is injurious to his society—is prohibited. Only Almighty Allah can possess the omniscient wisdom to know in absolute terms what is beneficial and what is harmful for the life of human individuals and their society, since men, even the wisest or best of them, are bound by a limited human understanding and perspective. In any case, if something is prohibited, many harmless and beneficial alternatives have been provided among permissible things in its place, thus enabling human beings to satisfy their needs and desires without resorting to impure, harmful or injurious things or behaviours.

Now what precisely are the Islamic teachings relating to morals and behaviour? In many respects they resemble the teachings of Judaism and Christianity, a fact which one would naturally expect since the messages brought by Moses, Jusus, Muhammad and all the other prophets (peace be on them all), who are referred to in the Qur'an as "*Muslims*," that is, those who submit to Allah, was one and the same: the message of surrender to Allah's will and guidance. But the Islamic teachings, as we shall see, go many steps further, embracing the whole of man's individual and collective life in all its aspects—personal, social, political and economic, as well as what pertains to the spiritual life—thus providing alike for the needs of his body, mind and soul. They include the rights which an individual owes to himself, the rights which he owes to Allah, and the rights which he owes to others. In many ways the Islamic teachings are also far more clear and specific. Rather than merely laying down broad general principles such as "Be kind" or "Be honest," clear illustrations provided in the Qur'an and in the Prophet's *Sunnah* demonstrate what being kind and honest mean in practical terms; that is, the concrete behaviours appropriate to various situations which embody the virtues which Islam inculcates in the Muslim's personality are clearly defined and delineated.

Islam proclaims that the guidance contained in the Qur'an is final, permanent and binding on all people of all times and places. Consequently, regardless of how much time may pass and to what extent the habits and living patterns of people may change, the principles of Islam—its standards, values and injunctions—are not subject to change no matter what the prevalent values of the society or the opinion of the majority may happen to be. In Islam the consensus of the majority or the desires of men can never alter a Divine principle or law, or make right wrong or wrong right, for this is the prerogative of Allah alone. This does not, of course, in any sense imply that Islam is against change or that it wants a static society, but it does mean that its laws for governing human behaviour constitute permanent and unalterable spiritual principles within the framework of which man is to order his life; as such, they are not time-bound nor subject to alteration. Thus, while there will naturally be vast changes in people's life-styles and ways of doing things with the passing of time, the principles and laws of Islam may not be altered, "modernized," "reformed" or in any way made conformable to the desires of the people since they come from the Lord of the people, not for their pleasure or convenience but for their permanent well-being and utmost good.

In order to put the Islamic teachings relating to morals and behaviour into a clearer perspective, we have listed below a number of Islamic injunctions and prohibitions. Obeying the injunctions is considered a virtue, while doing what is prohibited constitutes disobedience to Allah and a sin. As will be seen, there is considerable overlapping between the vlaues/attitudes we discussed in the preceding section, and morals and their actualisation in behaviour. Taken all together, this should enable us to build a clear understanding of the kind of person Islam wants the Muslim to be, what moral principles it wants him to live by, and how it wants him to behave.

Commands and Injunctions	Prohibitions
Consciousness and fear of Allah (*taqwa*) are to govern all a Muslim's behaviour; the acts of worship are a means to this end.	The Muslim is never supposed to lose sight of his relationship and responsibility to Allah, nor to act in violation of it.
Self-discipline and self-control are essential to a Muslim's character and behaviour.	Undisciplined desires, over-indulgence in physical appetites and luxuries, uncontrolled passions, harshness and a bad temper are considered detestable.
Truthfulness, reliability and honesty both in character and in behaviour, and the keeping of promises, commitments and trusts are required.	Lying, cheating, failing to keep promises and trusts and any type of dishonest dealing are strictly prohibited.

Commands and Injunctions

To be just and fair, even at the expense of one's own self or one's family is required on an individual level. The Islamic society is also required to adhere very strictly to justice in all affairs.

All human life is sacred to Muslims, and upholding its sanctity is an Islamic obligation.

Forgiveness for personal injuries inflicted by others is enjoined. If the injured person or his immediate relatives choose not to forgive, however, they have the right to retaliation. This is not to exceed the injury done and is not to be inflicted upon any one except the guilty person himself; a monetary settlement is also acceptable in place of physical retaliation.

The Muslim is supposed to resist injustice, tyranny and oppression: both of himself and others, by every means in his power: with his hand, with his tongue, and within his heart.

Respect for the property and possessions of others, as for one's own, is required. In a

Prohibitions

Injustice and unfairness in any form are very strongly condemned. The Islamic society is not permitted to perpetrate injustice upon human beings in any form.

Killing except in self-defense or in a righteous war is one of the greatest sins. Life may be taken by the state only after due process of law for capital crimes (see page (119).

Revenge and blood-feuding are prohibited and are considered serious sins; equal retaliation constitutes justice, while revenge is a willful transgression of justice and defiance of the authority of the law.

Tyranny and oppression of any of Allah's creatures, including by a ruler or government, are very strictly prohibited and constitute very grave sins.

Stealing is prohibited and is severely punished. However, the punishment is to be applied only

Commands and Injunctions

society in which *zakat* is in effect, and where widespread voluntary Charity is practiced, stealing due to poverty becomes unnecessary and criminal.

Purity, modesty and decency in behaviour, appearance, dress and speech are required. The dignity and honour of women is very strongly stressed. Marriage is very much encouraged, providing a permissible and sanctioned outlet for sexual needs.

Responsible and harmonious relations between husband and wife, proper care, maintenance and training of children are strongly stressed.

Obedience, respect and kind treatment of parents, and kindly, responsible relations with relatives are of the greatest importance.

Neighborliness, helpfulness and kindliness in all spheres of life, and to all people, are enjoined.

Respect for the honour, reputation and privacy of others is required.

Prohibitions

in cases of deliberate theft, not theft due to hunger or want (see page 119).

Free mixing between men and women, and any form of physical contact outside marriage are prohibited. A woman's beauty and sexual attributes are not for public display. Fornication, adultery, prostitution and homosexuality are not merely personal sins but also very serious crimes which attack the foundations of a wholesome society, and they carry extremely grave penalties.

Lack of responsibility, cruelty or harshness toward one's spouse or children are very condemnable.

Disobedience, dishonour or harshness toward parents are among the worst of sins. Breaking ties of relationship with kin is disliked.

Hard-heartedness, unkindness and bad behaviour to others are detested.

Gossiping, back-biting, prying into others' affairs, suspicion, violating others' privacy are prohibited.

Commands and Injunctions

Kindness to animals, respect for all of Allah's creation are enjoined. If an animal is to be killed, it must be done swiftly and in a merciful manner.

Ownership of property, trade and business are permissible and encouraged. Money is to remain in circulation through useful investment or spending. Work and constructive effort of all kinds are encouraged.

Spending in a reasonable manner on oneself or one's family is permissible. Generosity and hospitality are strongly enjoined. The right of the poor and distressed on one's wealth is to be remembered.

Enjoyment, in moderation, of Allah's wholesome gifts of food and drink is permissible.

Cooperation for good, enjoining what is right and forbidding what is wrong, are obligations. The Muslim of any walk of life or calling is to feel a sense of responsibility for the state of his society and its affairs.

Prohibitions

Torture or cruelty to animals of any kind and wanton destruction of nature are prohibited.

Gaining wealth by interest, bribery or gambling is prohibited. The society is to flourish by cooperation and mutual help, not by the exploitation of some people by others. Any economic practice which harms the people or the society, including working in prohibited trades (see page 160), is forbidden.

Excessive love of wealth or possessions, miserliness, hoarding, spending for unreasonable luxuries and wastefulness are all prohibited. Material things are not to become a preoccupation or one's goal in life.

Gluttony and over-indulgence in food or drink are disliked. The use of alcohol, intoxicating drugs and pork is prohibited.

Cooperating for evil purposes is prohibited, and lack of concern or failure to try to change what is wrong are breaches of responsibility.

It will be clear from the foregoing how far-reaching and comprehensive the Islamic moral injunctions are, applying just as much to the social, political, legal, administrative and economic affairs of the Muslim society as they do to the individual Muslim's relationship with Allah or with his family and friends. This is because Islam views human life as an indivisible, unified whole which cannot be broken up into unrelated parts. Consequently, notions such as "the separation of church and state" or "rendering unto Allah what is Allah's and unto Caesar what is Caesar's" do not fit and have no relevance when applied to Islam, for they pertain to a religion or ideology in which the various elements of life are considered to be separate from each other, with different criteria applied to each. In Islam there is no church establishment, no priesthood (for, the Islamic scholars, religion teachers, *imams* and other religious functionaries are simply persons who are well-versed in Islamic knowledge, not priests; they are not ordained or regarded as divinely-appointed, or as having any special or intermediary status with Allah, and no notion of one part of life being for Allah and the Hereafter and another part being for the world, since all of man's life is for Allah and for Him, alone.

What the Islamic teachings actually accomplish is to make man into an integrated, unified being, giving his life the form and direction which its Creator wants it to have. The Qur'an tells us that although man has been created in the best of moulds and his nature is higher than even that of the Angels, in order to reach this potential he must submit to Allah's guidance and strive to his utmost. The function of the Islamic teachings, therefore, is to work with man's extremely complex, multi-faceted nature, with its components of body, mind and soul, and bring it under one jurisdiction so to speak. Instead of either denying the animal part of man or suppressing it altogether, or alternatively allowing it unlimited freedom, Islam directs and channelizes such needs and desires so that they can be expressed in a manner which is constructive and beneficial rather than in a random, uncontrolled manner which can destroy man and his society. For example, Islam does not condemn or deny man's sexual needs but insists that expressions of human sexuality be limited to a particular use under specified conditions: that is, only in the married state as part of a total relationship of mutual commitment and responsibility. Again, it takes another basic element of human nature, the desire for gain and material possessions, establishing such limits and direction for it as will keep the Muslim from losing his perspective and becoming greedy, miserly, self-indulgent or preoccupied with material things. Islam insists, in short, that the human being be truly *human*, not an animal or a devil who has lost all sense of perspective in the pursuit of his uncontrolled, undirected aims and desires.

SECTION THREE:

The Collective Aspect

firmly rooted in acknowledgement of the Creator, acceptance of man's accountability to Him, and simultaneous recognition of His sole right to legislate for His creatures and their obligation to obey Him, the resemblance of any concept or system to Islam is obviously a superficial one.

The point to be borne in mind is that the principles on which the Islamic systems are based are constant, unalterable and universal ones originating in Divine revelation. However, the details of their application may certainly be adjusted as necessary within the Islamic framework to fit existing needs and circumstances. Hence, while Muslims are unquestionably permitted to adopt useful and beneficial knowledge and technology from any source, they are not to do this blindly. In concrete terms, if they make use of a technology from a non-Islamic source, they are permitted to accept only the technology itself, not the concepts, values or behaviour of the society from which it originates, nor anything related to its application which is contrary to Islamic values and laws. The technology, which is a practical, concrete thing, is then assimilated into the total Islamic framework of the society, acquiring its own Islamic emphasiz and perspective so that it can be a source of benefit, not of harm or disruption of values and societal patterns. For the mission of the Islamic society is not to imitate others' concepts, life-styles or habits but rather to be the leader and example to other societies, particularly in the area of spiritual and moral values.

✳✳✳✳✳

In discussing the collective aspects of human interaction in any society, it is only logical to start at the beginning—that is, with the family. The Islamic teachings are designed to strengthen and protect this precious nurturing ground of future generations with the utmost care and concern. However, in Islam "family" does not dencte merely the nuclear family of Western society but includes, in addition to husband, wife and children, other close relatives as well. This of course does not mean that all the relatives must live together under one roof or even near each other but that, even if they are scattered and geographically distant, they recognize their

ISLAM IN SOCIETY

Our next step will be to take a look at how the Islamic teachings are applied to the collective aspects of human life. It is not our intention here to either discuss any existing societies or to set up a model for an Islamic society, but simply to convey some idea of how Islam regulates various aspects of human interaction and to make some observations as to how this may be implemented in practice.

As we have already seen, Islam possesses its own social, political, legal and economic concepts and systems, all of which have their base in the Qur'an and the Prophet's *Sunnah*. While these may have some points of similarity to the concepts and systems of other societies or ideologies, they are in fact unique and distinctive to Islam and cannot be forced into the mould of this or that man-made system or philosophy. It is important to bear in mind that by the time the revelation of the Qur'an had been completed in the year 632 After Christ, the principles governing these concepts and systems had been laid down in complete form. Hence the Islamic concepts and systems had been laid down in complete form. Hence the Islamic concepts and systems—whether they relate to political, economic, legal or social aspects—pre-date the development of modern systems in any part of the world by several hundred years. Any apparent similarities between Islam and other systems cannot, therefore, possibly by due to Islam's "borrowing" from them but rather to the "borrowing" of other systems from Islam, or, more logically, to the fact that Islam's principles and laws are so obviously correct and workable that they would ultimately have been discovered by thinkers in other systems with or without any borrowing having taken place. In actual fact, the similarities between the Islamic principles and other systems are more apparent than real, for unless a system is membership in a unit whose numbers are bound together by ties of blood and mutual responsibility.

In Islam marriage, which is the cornerstone of the family, is very strongly encouraged; in fact, it is mentioned in a *Hadith* of the Prophet (peace be on him) as being the second half or completion of one's faith. The purpose of marriage in Islam is that a man and woman build a home, live together in love, kindness, mutual sympathy, support and companionship, meet one another's sexual needs, and rear children together. By their marriage they form a new family unit which also supports and strengthens the existing families of the pair. Marriage is seen as a working partnership, with each partner assuming responsibility for their common life together.

Islam recognizes that men and women have different natures, strengths and weaknesses, and hence it assigns different but complementary roles within the society to each, dividing the total work which must be done for the process of living between them in a way which best suits their innate capacities and natures. Within the family group, Islam assigns the leadership role to men, together with financial responsibility for its members; the support and maintenance of the women and children are their concern. Women in turn are responsible for looking after their husbands, comfort and well-being, guarding their honour and administering their properties, providing for the physical and emotional well-being of their children, and, with their husbands' help rearing them in the best possible way as sound Muslims. Although as a matter of convenience most women do the work of their households, this is not required by Islam, and a woman is perfectly free to turn over all or part of the domestic work to others, as circumstances permit, and to pursue her own work or interests, provided the family— particularly in the area of the training of children—is not neglected.

Islam lays great stress on the importance and desirability of having children and makes raising them properly a matter of vital concern. At the same time, young people are required to develop a sense of responsibility for their own conduct quite early in life. A young Muslim is considered by Islam as accountable for his or her own actions by the age of puberty (that is, by the age of eleven to sixteen years), by which time an individual is considered to be capable of possessing an adequate understanding of the Islamic teachings and of what is permissible and prohibited, as well as a sound practice of its various aspects. Children are reared with the understanding that the values and behaviours they are taught are not simply their parents' but Allah's, and that they apply as much to their parents and all other members of society as to themselves, while the parents, for their part, are expected to provide a sound example for them to follow. Consequently there is a continuity of values from generation to generation, and rebellion against them is not merely a rebellion against parental standards but against Allah. As a result, while the drive for independence naturally exists among maturing Muslim youth, rather than being a time of crisis, rebellion or deviation from accepted norms, adolescence is rather a time for serious preparation and adjustment to the assumption of adult responsibility.

Islam also requires that Muslims take responsibility for their parents when they become elderly, or for other aged relatives who may need their care or support. In an Islamic society, the phenomenon of a single woman or old person living alone is virtually unknown; such people are to be part of someone's household where their material wants and need for love, care and companionship can be met in a humane manner. Women's right to maintenance by the men of their families (their husbands, or if they are single, widowed or divorced, their fathers, brothers, adult sons or some other male relative) protects them from having to go out and struggle to earn a living the best they can, although they may lack marketable skills and work opportunities compatible with the dignity of women, in addition to the problem of the care and rearing of their children. Muslim women may own property, engage in business or work, but even in this case they are not required to provide for the family's maintenance because Islam has made this the responsibility of men.

Partly in order to provide a home and maintenance for every woman in the society and partly in order to make provision for other special situations, Islam permits Muslim men to marry more than one wife. This provision for limited polygamy is not, as some imagine, a recommendation or encouragement to plural marriage, or a blanket permission to marry more than one woman and then treat the wives any way one likes. Rather the permission to contract marriage with more than one woman is contingent upon the observance of scrupulous fairness among the wives. In the words of the Qur'an:

> "And if you fear that you will not deal justly by orphans, marry of the women who seem good to you two or three or four. And if you fear that you cannot do justice, then (only) one...."   (4:3)

> "You will not be able to deal equally between wives however much you desire (to do so). But (if you have more than one wife) do not turn altogether away (from one), leaving her as in suspense...."   (4:129)

This does not of course mean that a man must love his wives equally—an obvious impossibility since no one can order his emotions—but that he should provide them with equal facilities and maintenance, spend an equal amount of time with each, and not give them the feeling that he prefers one over the other. This is clearly no easy task for the average man. Yet because Islam recognizes the nature and needs of women, and does not want them to live alone to bear all the economic and other burdens of life on their shoulders, or to spend their lives without the love and care of a husband or the blessing of children; because it takes into cognizance that there are unusual situations such as barrenness or chronic illness in women which might make marrying more than one wife desirable, the permission for plural marriages has been given. For example, after a war the number of women is often much greater than that of men and many women are helpless and destitute. The Islamic solution—the human, dignified and natural solution—is that a man should, under such conditions, shoulder the responsibility for more than one wife and provide for these homeless ones rather than their being forced to struggle alone in order to survive, often being reduced to prostitution because they can find no other means of livelihood. While it is unfortunately true that in practice the Islamic provision for polygamy has sometimes been misused, this does not change the wisdom of this

provision, the result of which in past times was to stabilise Muslim
societies by making it possible for every single individual to marry
and have a home in one way or another. Moreover; with such a
provision there is no excuse for anyone, man or woman, to resort
to illicit relationships to satisfy his/her sexual needs. However, no
matter how fair a husband may try to be with his wives, there are
obvious problems of rivalry and jealousy in plural marriages, and
thus, while the provision for polygamy makes the social system
flexible enough to deal with all kinds of conditions, it is not
necessarily recommended or preferred by Islam.[1]

While divorce is allowed, the Prophet (peace be on him) said
that of all the things which Allah has permitted, divorce is the most
hated by Him. This in itself points to the grave undesirability of
divorce except as a last resort when all means of reconciliation
between husband and wife fail. Such means include the attempts
of relatives and friends to mediate between the two to help them
resolve their differences. Effective safeguards are also built into
the divorce procedure so that at any stage short of the final
pronouncement reconciliation between the two parties can take
place. When divorce does occur, however, it is not hedged about
by difficulties or by long-drawn-out court procedures with mutual
recriminations or fights over the custody of children, nor is a man
penalised by having to support his former wife for the remainder
of his life even though he may not have been at fault in any way.
In any case, divorce is in fact an infrequent occurrence among
Muslims. Although the two partners as a rule do not know each
other before marriage since Islam totally prohibits such things as
dating or pre-marital intimacy, the fact the Muslim marriages are
based on common beliefs, values, ways of life and submission to
Allah's commands rather than on romantic attachment before
marriage provides them with a strong and sound foundation for
building a life together.

---

1. Here the Prophet's own example is instructive and inspiring. He was
   married to one woman, his first wife Khadijah, for twenty-five years,
   living with her in the greatest harmony and tenderness. Only after her
   death after he reached the age of fifty, did he contract other marriages,
   each one to cement friendships, promote alliances or teach some essential
   lesson to his community, and to provide a vital example to Muslims of
   how to treat one's spouses under the varied conditions of life.

As we have seen, absolute chastity before marriage and absolute fidelity to one's mate is required of both men and women. Islam considers the honour of women sacred and insists that they be treated with appropriate dignity and respect, and for their part they are required to guard their modesty and purity with utmost care. An Islamic society is to be free of the degradation of women and the exploitation of their sexuality, whether by men or by commercial interests, and of any influences which weaken marriage, the family or people's morals. Thus Islam establishes certain limits to govern the relations between men and women so that the interaction of Muslims may be characterized by absolute integrity, openness, purity and honesty; these will be discussed in detail on pages 163-169.

Muslims traditionally address one another as "brother" and "sister" and attempt to behave as befits such a relationship. Responsibility may be said to be the keynote of all relationships and interaction among them, and the rights of others and one's obligations toward them are universally acknowledged. Cooperation is the rule rather than competition; in fact, competition should consist of trying to excel in being and doing good rather than in outdoing others in acquiring possessions, status or other such aspects of life. Unity of purpose and action, mutual helpfulness and working together are very strongly stressed.

In Islam helpfulness and concern for others preclude such practices as dealing in interest which takes advantage of other's needs and permits an increase in the wealth of the lender of money without his working for it, whether it is done by an individual or a financial institution such as a bank, and Muslims are expected to develop and implement a sound, workable alternative interest-free economic system. Neither are any sorts of commercial interests permitted to exploit the people, whether it be by exciting greed and materialsim through advertising, by the manufacture of goods which are harmful or undesirable, or by ecologically-unsound practices which wantonly destroy irreplaceable natural resources for easily dispensed-with consumer goods. Wastage, whether of wealth or of natural resources, is prohibited; instead, the resources given by Allah are to be treated with respect and utilised in the best way possible for the welfare of all, with an eye to the future as well as the present.

The material development of the society, whether by industrialisation, utilisation of resources, the application of science and technology, or other means is considered a religious obligation in Islam. However, the aim of all such efforts must be the welfare of the people and the society, keeping in mind the needs of future generations as well, never the enrichment of individuals or interest groups. Hence new developments under consideration in an Islamic society might be studied by panels of experts in various fields, including Islamic sociologists and psychologists, to determine their probable long-range effects on the society, and they would be undertaken or dropped on the basis of their recommendations. Random and too rapid development, which destroys religious and societal values and stable living patterns, would not be permitted, and moderation in production and consumption patterns would be stressed.

The charitableness which is so central to the feeling of love and Brotherhood among Muslims is intended to equalize the wealth in the society so that some people are not excessively rich while others are destitute. Every Muslim is expected to feel and to accept responsibility for those who are near to him, and even for others who are outside his immediate circle. Thus orphans are as a rule brought up by relatives, not adopted by strangers or put into institutions, and as we have mentioned, a similar responsibility is assumed for the aged and for single, widowed or divorced women, either by their relatives or through plural marriages. To put it another way, in the Islamic society, kindness, charitableness and help to the needy and unfortunate are personalised rather than institutionalised; that is, such help is not merely the duty of the government but is the responsibility of every Muslim toward whomever is within his reach as far as his means allow, although the government is required to do its part by collecting and distributing *zakat* and by any additional means, such as the levying of taxes and duties, it may consider necessary.

In any group of three or more Muslims, one is selected by them as the leader; this applies not only to a group which has gathered for *salat* and to the family but to any collection of individuals, including the Islamic society and state. Since the people have deputed authority to the leader, they have the obligation to follow his leadership and instructions even if they disagree with him,[2] provided he does not ask them to do anything which involves disobedience to Allah. However, if he does not fulfil his responsibilities, does not follow the teachings of Islam either in his personal life or in the conduct of the affairs of state, or asks the people to disobey Allah's laws, he must be replaced by a more responsible person. In Islam the leader or head of state has no special prerogatives or privileges but rather only graver responsibilities for which he will be held accountable to Allah; he is in office not for his own aggrandisement but to serve the people. He is therefore required to consult with the people and to consider their needs and well-being in all matters.[3] An Islamic government therefore embodies the dual principles of obedience to the leader and the leader's obligation to consult with the people concerning the conduct of affairs.[4] Moreover, no legislation is to be enacted which is contrary to the Qur'an or the Prophet's *Sunnah*, and all legislation which is enacted is to be in conformity with these two sources of Islamic legislation. In matters concerning which Islam is silent, the government is of course free to enact whatever legislation it deems necessary within the general framework of the laws and values of Islam.

An Islamic government is responsible for providing an environment which will make it easy for Muslims to practice Islam and difficult for them to deviate from it. Any establishments which thrive on immoral or prohibited activities such as those related to prostitution and other forms of sexual license, gambling, dinking, etc., would

---

2. This is the first fundamental principle for the conduct of government in Islam, that of obedience to the *ameer* (the leader or head of state).

3. The second principle is that *shura* or mutual consulation between the *Ameer* and the people.

4. Islam does not lay down a particular method for the selection of the leader. However, his selection by the consent of the people and the evidence of their willingness to follow his leadership are fundamental principles.

not be permitted; manufacture and sale of alcoholic beverages, drug traffic and pornographic literature would be illegal; and the public media would not be allowed to portray or describe anything leading toward sexual immorality, vice and Crime. In principle, any whole-some and permissible outlets and recreations which do not conflict with Islamic goals and values would be encouraged and proper facilities for them provided. The modesty and dignity of women would be safeguarded by encouraging modest dress, providing separate facilities wherever necessary (secondary schools and colleges, medical and recreational facilities, etc.), and taking stern measures against those who in any way annoy or molest women.

Seeking knowledge is considered a religious obligation in Islam, and Education for both children and adults would be strongly stressed. Schools would combine secular and Islamic studies into one curriculum through secondary level in order to provide a comprehensive and integrated approach. A very broad-based religious Education would be included which would not only offer Islamic studies but the study of other religions, systems, ideologies and cultures. A sense of pride in one's Islamic identity and heritage would be stressed. Young people would be given assistance in marrying early, if they desired, so that their sexual needs could be met without resort to illicit relations. Preparation and training for parenthood would be made available to them, and parents would be given every support and assistance in rearing their children properly. Women would be encouraged to obtain higher educations to prepare them both to be effective homemakers and mothers and for other essential work, particularly in the educational, medical, nursing and social work fields, and accommodations in schedule and leave would be made for working women to enable them to take care of the needs of their families and for such situations as pregnancy, childbirth, illness in the family, etc.

Justice before the law would be strictly impartial without regard to religion, race, position, wealth or any other criteria; the head of state, officials and members of the most influential families would be just as subject to its provisions as the most humble members of society. In this context it may be remarked that every individual in a society has a certain basic responsibility to that society not to transgress against its established limits, which relate to the sanctity of life, person, property and sexual inviolability. In turn each society has its own system of penalties for violating such limits which stem from its basic understanding of human responsibility and interaction. In a society in which the majority of people are Muslims, that is, accepting the limits laid down by Almighty Allah, crimes would be dealt with by the punishments prescribed by Islam.[5] Islam maintains that the violation of these

---

5   While such punishments as the execution of those who commit premeditated murder or robbery with murder, cutting off the fingers or hand of a habitual thief (this excludes those who steal due to poverty), the stoning of adulterers (only after guilt has been unquestionably established in court by four eye-witnesses to the act or by self-confession, which means in effect that the punishment is virtually never carried out), or the public lashing of fornicators or drinkers may seem harsh to many people who are accustomed to living in societies in which such violations of moral codes are so common as to be taken as a normal and necessary condition of life, the Islamic view is that these constitute very serious and criminal offenses against morality and the social order, and are neither necessary nor to be tolerated. Hence the Islmaic punishments, called in Arabic *hudood*, that is, the "limits" imposed by Allah, are not in fact intended merely as penalties for a proven Crime but as deterrents against further Crime. As a result, in those societies in which the punishments prescribed by the Islamic *Shar'iah* are enforced, there is little or no Crime, and citizens feel safe, protected by a law so strict that virtually no one dares to risk transgressing it. To those who argue that such penalties are harsh and do not show compassion to criminals, Islam's answer is that the criminal's own lack of compassion in violating an innocent victim has forfeited him the right to be treated indulgently by society. It sees failure to administer adequate punishments to violators of moral codes as the ultimate injustice to the people of the society. That in many places people cannot walk alone in the streets due to fear of rape or robbery, and that they cannot feel safe even in securely locked houses, may be very "fair" to criminals but it is assuredly not fair to those who live in constant fear of attack. Crime is to be dealt with at its source by eliminating the problems which lead people to it, whether these are lack of a sense of responsibility to Allah and to other human beings, emotional insecurity, economic frustrations, injustice, etc., rather than by encouraging Crime through failure to provide adequate deterrents. See the leading article. "Moslem Justice." *Wall Street Journal*. May 11, 1979.

limits, which are known to all, calls for such exemplary punishment that others will be effectively deterred from committing similar acts.

Freedom of religion and conscience for non-Muslims living in the Islamic state is a fundamental principle of Islam, including the freedom to practice the rites of their respective faiths. The Qur'an commands explicitly, "Let there be no compulsion in religion" (2:256), for one's religious beliefs are obviously a matter of inner conviction and cannot be imposed from outside, nor does anyone have the right to impose them since Allah gives each human individual freedom to choose them for himself.[6] Islam also guarantees all other basic freedoms to all persons in an Islamic state without any distinction or discrimination on the basis of religion, race, national origin, etc. In such a state every citizen would be guaranteed such rights as protection of person, property and honour, justice before the law on an equal basis with all other citizens, ownership of private property, the right to engage in business or investment beneficial to society, to select his/her own marriage partner, to acquire an Education, to travel, and to do any lawful work of his own choice. Although the head of the Islamic state would be definition be a Muslim, non-Muslims would by guaranteed adequate representation and would be able to hold positions of importance in the society. Non-Muslims, like Muslims themselves, would obviously not be permitted to carry on activities which are prohibited or undermining to morals and social stability, and no one would be permitted to propagate Atheism or godless, violent ideologies such as Communism or to engage in political activities related to them.

---

6   The fact that there are many places in the Muslim world today where small groups of non-Muslims live and carry on their religious practices and traditions without hindrance in the midst of the Muslim majority should be sufficient proof that "Conversion by the sword" is a fiction, for Islam strictly prohibits forced conversions. An additional proof to which history bears witness is the fact that on occasion Muslim armies were welcomed with joy and relief by non-Muslim peoples living under oppressive rulers, who knew that Muslims, although professing a different fiath, would govern them with a tolerance and justice which they often could not obtain from their own co-religionists.

As has already been mentioned, *jihad* is an obligation on the individual Muslim, and it is an obligation on the Islamic society as well. Unfortunately the word *jihad* has been represented so often in the Western media (and by some well-meaning but ignorant Muslims as well) as meaning "holy war" that this is now accepted as its real meaning. This is totally incorrect, for *jihad* simply means "striving," as any native speaker of Arabic can verify. The first and most essential *jihad* which the Muslim must carry on is within himself in a never-ceasing effort at self-improvement and self-purification. This is known as *jihad bil nafs* (striving within the self), which the Prophet, peace be on him, called "the greatest *jihad.*" This unremitting struggle is to begin within the Muslim's soul from the time he or she attains a consciousness of right and wrong, and it does not end until the end of life itself

In addition to this, Islam makes it a duty on Muslims to reach out into society and carry on the struggle, by any means in their power both on an individual and collective level, against all forms of evil and corruption; they are also required to wage an unremitting war on injustice, tyranny and oppression. Such *jihad fi sabeel Allah* (striving in the path of Allah) is to be carried on by the tongue, by the pen, and, if these fail, by the hand as a last resort, Islam absolutely prohibits Muslims to perpetrate injustice, aggression or harm on others; it also enjoins forgiveness and forbearance in the case of personal wrongs done to themselves. At the same time, they are not permitted to allow themselves or others to become the passive victims of other's injustice or aggression which, if they are not checked, will become more and more menacing to human dignity and freedom. The Qur'an says:

> "Permission is given to those who fight because they have been wronged, and indeed Allah is able to give them victory: those who have been driven from their homes unjustly only because they said, 'Our Lord is Allah.' For had it not been for Allah's repelling some men by means of others, cloisters and churches and oratories and mosques, in which the name of Allah is often mentioned, would assuredly have been pulled down. And lo! Allah helps one who helps Him. For verily, Allah is Strong, Powerful."
> (22:39-40)

A *Hadith* of the Prophet (peace be on him) further clarifies this point. He instructed some of his companions, "Help your brother, whether he is the oppressor or the oppressed." When they asked him how they could help one who was an oppressor, he said, "Restrain him from it." Thus the Muslim is not only-required to give assistance to one who is the victim of tyranny, injustice and wrong-doing, whether he is a Muslim or a non-Muslim, a single individual or a whole people, but also to try to stop the one who is committing it and to strive with all his energies to bring about the rule of righteousness, freedom and justice for all people.

*****

A society such as the one we have just finished describing would be one which, if it existed, would be as nearly ideal in moral and human terms as it is possible for a society to be. It would long ago have won the admiration of all sincere and concerned people and would have attained the moral leadership of the world. The question may now rightly be asked: "Where is such a society? If Islam is all you say it is, why don't we see societies like this throughout the Muslim world? Doesn't this prove that Islam cannot be all you say? Besides this, we know some Muslims. Perhaps a very few of them may be something like what you have described but the rest are just regular people, not especially good in any way or even really different from other people, and some of them are even worse. In the face of all the claims and counter-claims we are hearing today about Islam, how can we know whether what you are saying is correct or what the critics and opponents of Islam say?"

These are very relevant questions, questions which any person who wants to understand Islam and Muslims is entitled to have answered in an honest and straight-forward manner. It is readily apparent that Islam—or any other religion—can be effective in people's lives only to the extent that they practice it. And there are as many kinds of Muslims in the world today as there are followers of any other religion. As there are Jews and Christians and Hindus and Buddhists who are totally committed to their faiths and others who are nominal followers—the "Sunday" or "Christmas-and-

Easter Christians," or less than that—so there are Muslims of varying degrees of conviction and practice of Islam. On forms and applications, in the space where one is asked to state his religion, all of these alike write the name of the faith into which they were born, but this is merely a cold and meaningless statistic which says nothing at all about their degree of understanding, conviction and commitment to their faith.

The answers to these questions are inextricably connected with the present situation of the Muslim world, and in the section which follows, we will attempt, in the briefest possible form, to give some idea concerning this very complex subject. The point to be borne in mind is that the Muslims who come from it to America or other countries of the West *are* the Muslim world in miniature; one can find representives of its types in every shade and degree. If all, or even most, Muslims were true in word and deed to the religion which they profess, there would be no need to write these lines. Everyone is aware of the extreme greed, materialsim and decadence of some of the newly-rich Arabs, of the total lack of Islamic values and behaviour of many other "Muslims" from various parts of the East, and some people find it revolting. If these are Muslims, one may ask, what kind of religion is Islam?

Yes, it is undoubtedly true that all these people call themselves Muslims, or at least that is what they say when asked what faith they profess. But if the reader has ever met a true Muslim, whether he or she is an Arab or a Pakistani or Turk or African or Indonesian or European or American or whatever it may be, he will certainly be aware of the difference between a Muslim by name and a Muslim by conviction, commitment and life. Yet even such sincere and committed Muslims sometimes do wrong or act out of character. And then *that* is also not Islam.

For Islam is a complete and perfect system of life revealed by Almighty Allah and exemplified in the life of His messenger. Muhammad (peace be on him), the totality of all the concepts, attitudes, values, moral guidelines, behaviours, worships and living patterns we have been talking about in these pages and much, much more. It remains so just as much today as when it was first proclaimed on earth, its validity and truth totally independent of whether Muslims practice it faithfully or fail to practice it, now or in the past or in the future. It is therefore essential to maintain a clear distinction in our minds between what Islam is and what Muslims are, between the religion itself and the people who profess it, and if the behaviour which we observe among Muslims does not correctly reflect Islam, to draw our conclusions concerning the individual Muslims themselves rather than concerning the religion which they profess but do not necessarily practice in a faithful and conscientious manner.

ISLAM AND THE MUSLIM WORLD

In order to understand what is happening to Muslims, it is necessary to have a look at what is happening to the Muslim world. During the past century-and-a-half, the entire world has gone through tremendous upheavals, particularly in the realm of religion and values. While Europe and America were experiencing a profound loss of belief in religion, due in part to the irreconcilable conflict between science and what was supposed to be the "revealed Word" and in part to changes in people's values and outlooks as a result of massive changes in technology and patterns of living, the Muslim world too was experiencing a great crisis in the realm of religion and values.

During this period, due to a complex interplay of forces, while the hold of Christianity was weakening in the West, the influence of Islam was also becoming attenuated in the East. As a result, many Muslims so far lost sight of the true reality of their faith that masses of them took the traditions of their societies, some of which were from Islam and others from sources other than Islam, to be Islam itself. Their understanding of Islam as a dynamic, revolutionary system of life shrank until all that remained to them of it was a set of confused, quasi-Islamic traditions, some faded remnants of Islamic values and behaviour, and perhaps (but often not even that) praying and fasting in Ramadan, reading the Qur'an when someone died, and celebrating the 'Eids. Others went to the opposite extreme, placing great emphasiz on the worship aspects of Islam while ignoring all the rest of its teachings, especially in the area of striving, seeking knowledge, developing resources, political responsibility, cleanliness, etc. Muslim children living in areas outside the Arab world learned from pious but often ignorant teachers to pronounce the words of the Qur'an without understanding anything of their meaning, much less living by them, while in other places, youngsters grew up still more ignorant of Islam, believing it to be something related to the older generation which one is supposed to respect but which has no relevance or place in contemporary life.

At the same time, the Western influence emerged in the Muslim world and little by little grew stronger and stronger. In the past this trend was fueled by Western imperialism and the presence of Western officials, as well as by Christian missionaries and westernized, often Western-educated, natives who had returned home from a sojourn in Europe or America. Later industrial and commercial interests, finding a ready market for Western goods and expertise in Muslim countries, enthusiastically accelerated the process. Muslims became uneasily conscious of their own material backwardness and lack of modernity in comparison with the West, assisted by contact with Western goods and the lure of its life-styles, conveyed to every part of the globe by Western movies, media and propaganda. The West was seen as a glamorous utopia, and adoption of some of the trappings of its culture was looked upon as the instant way to modernization and progress. Unfortunately, what was adopted were not the outstanding and excellent aspects of Western culture but only the most superficial and harmful ones, which were simultaneously applauded by many on-lookers in the West as obvious signs that the Muslim world was now beginning to wake up and come of age: the old equation of bars, boogie and bikinis with progress and modernity. Under the impact of all this, many Muslims accepted Western society's dictum that religion, moral values and the pursuit of meaning be given no serious emphasiz or importance in society. Its criteria of being civilized— material advancement and the discarding of traditional values— were accepted by them as the true measure of the greatness of a society without their grasping the essential fact that genuine civilization must rest on a firm base of sound spiritual and moral principles, lacking which material progress simply becomes de-civilizing, dehumanising and destructive.

Consequently the present era has seen the emergence of three basic types of Muslims, who have their counterparts in other faiths as well. One is the individual for whom Islam is merely a vague tradition which more often than not he prefers to have nothing to do with, who inscribes himself "Muslim" on his passport simply because he is not a Christian or a Buddhist or anything else. He may either profess some outward tokens of respect for Islam or may reject it totally, but in any case it does not occur to him to guide his life by it or to try to practice it faithfully, and he regards those who do so as backward and stupid. This is understandable enough in view of the fact that almost invariably such individuals lack knowledge and understanding of Islam as a total world-view and system of life; moreover, they may never have been close to or even known anyone who could provide an example of real understanding and commitment to Islam. Such a "Muslim" may never have prayed in his life and may not even know how since he was not taught. For him Islam is simply a relic of ancient history. He may feel an occasional twinge of pride in his Islamic heritage when it is mentioned and may even come to the "defence" of Islam when it is attacked. Or he may think about it once in a while when someone dies ("Where am I going to go when this happens to me? Oh, well, Allah is merciful"), but he is too preoccupied with his daily activities and with his family and possessions and pleasures to follow up this train of thought. Many social problems and vices have by now crept into the lives of such Muslims, including an increasing incidence of divorce, sexual license, alcoholism, and total loss of values and direction. Basically they are Muslims-by-name, no different either in their concepts or behaviour from people who have no religion and no values, for in fact they have neither, and they are often very hostile to Islam and to Muslims who adhere to it faithfully.

The second group are the traditional Muslims. They may understand the basic concepts of Islam, may have some degree of Islamic knowledge and may follow the Islamic teachings to some extent but they do not understand it as a complete and dynamic system for all aspects of man's life nor do they adhere to its requirements in all aspects of their lives consistently and as a matter of principle and obligation. In their minds Islam is often intermixed with many pseudo-Islamic practices common to their societies, many of which are completely contrary to the Islamic teachings although they have acquired some sort of an "Islamic" sanction or flavour, and with many westernized ways of thought and behaviour as well. They definitely believe in Allah and Islam, but in a theoretical sort of way which does not carry enough conviction to move them steadily and consistently toward a totally Islamic orientation and way of life. Because they do not conceive of Islam as a complete system for all aspects of life, they are often critical of or look down on those who do as having "gone too far" in the matter of religion.

The third group consists of those Muslims who understand the religion they profess as a total system and who have consciously decided to pattern their lives according to it. Their world-view and frame of reference is that of Islam; their obedience, loyalty and devotion are for Allah alone; their goal is the Hereafter; and their community is the community of Believers. Many among this group are highly educated individuals who have arrived at such a position as a result of reflection on what is happening in the world around them. They are a unique group, part of the small yet strong company of true Believers in Allah who have been living in submission to Him since the first prophet, Adam (peace be on him), walked on earth, in obedience to His guidance.

Without question, to reach such a level of Islamic commitment requires an understanding which, due to very faulty and inadequate approaches to Islamic Education even in "Muslim" countries, few are able to attain. Moreover, the appeal of westernization and "modernity" is so strong that few people in the Muslim world have yet grasped the fact that material advancement is not necessarily the road to either true self-respect or satisfaction, and that it has not brought real happiness and well-being to the peoples of the West but instead a staggering array of societal and environmental problems because it has been divorced from the spiritual and moral dimensions which are as integral and essential a part of man's nature as in his material aspect.

When we survey the Muslim world today we see a confused and troubled picture in which political instability plays a major role. In spite of the Islamic requirement of a leader elected from among the people who consults with them in the conduct of affairs, in very few countries of the Muslim world today are there governments elected by the people and responsive to their needs, or capable of providing leadership and stability to their countries; rather there are, by and large, the rulers and the ruled. And although in most cases they professed Islam and often made a public show of piety, among the rulers of the Muslim world in recent years have been many who were dictators and oppressors of the most vicious sort. They stifled all criticism and dissent in their societies, whether by individuals, groups or the press, by sadistically oppressive means, making ruthless use of highly-trained secret police and intelligence services to suppress anyone they considered a threat to their unbridled power; they filled the prisons of their "Muslim" countries to overflowing with tens of thousands of sincere and committed Muslims, many belonging to the intelligentsia, who were trying to call for a revival of Islam in their societies or to question the policies or actions of the ruler. Hair-raising Nazi-style tortures were applied to countless numbers of them under which many died, and some of the best among them were executed for fabricated "crimes" in order to silence the voice of truth so the ruler might continue unimpeded in his relentless drive for absolute power.

Country after country in the Muslim world has seen rulers of this kind during the past half century or more, men who, although often "Muslims" themselves, hated and feared the very name of Islam because it constituted the only real challenge to their unchecked power and ambition, and who threw all their energies into trying to suppress it by oppressing Muslims. The Islamic requirement and demand of the people themselves for basic human freedoms, social justice and good rule were systematically and ruthlessly stifled. Any incident occurring under such conditions was blamed on Islam and "Muslim fanaticism," as if one had to be either a Muslim or a fanatic to want freedom and justice; indeed, incidents expressly manufactured by the government for the purpose of discrediting Muslims have not been unknown. But since Islam, which is deep within the life-blood of Muslims even though they may be indifferent to its requirements, could not be so easily dismissed, such rulers attempted to reduce it to mere piety and acts of worship lest it emerge as a strong, dynamic movement in which each individual feels a keen sense of responsibility for how the country is governed, what happens to its resources which belong to all the people, the morals and behaviour of its officials, and the entire host of matters over which governments have jurisdiction, which Almighty Allah has made the concern of every Muslim individual as a member of his society as well.

And what of the people in the face of all this? While Muslims of the first type are busy living the life of the world, preoccupied with their possessions, enjoyments, relationships and the increase of their material advantages, the second type of Muslims live in some half-way house between total loss of Islamic values and adherence to them, with various excuses and apologies for their lack of commitment. The Muslims in the third category stand firm on the Islamic principles and values, serving as a counterbalancing force against random "progress" and indiscriminate adoption of values and behaviours which are not appropriate for Muslims and can do great harm to their societies. Because of their certain and unwavering conviction of the truth of Islam, such individuals cannot be swayed in the direction of ideologies such as Communism as can others due to their basic lack of convictions, especially in the face of the multitude of economic, political and social problems facing their countries at the present time.

Today, in spite of all these difficult circumstances, a wave of Islamic consciousness and pride is being felt throughout the Muslim world. For many years the people of this area had been told in so many explicit and implicit ways that they were backward and inferior, and that the only way to rise out of this state was to discard their religion and traditions and adopt westernization; many believed this and are now following the path of crass materialsim. Others, having taken a good look at Western society, have become aware of its pitfalls and have grasped the fact that material progress and prosperity do not constitute the total fulfillment of man's nature nor provide him with the Paradise on earth which they seemed to promise. After one attains all that, they ask, then what? Prosperity can leave an individual as inwardly empty as poverty. Such people have come to the realization that human beings must, by the necessity of their *human* nature, concern themselves with something much more significant than merely the material sphere, with meaning and not simply with matter. As a result of all this, they have come to a deep and unshakable conviction that whatever is most precious, whatever is most essential to man's existence, is to be found in their fourteen-hundred-year-old Islamic heritage, in their religion and its way of life rather than in any other system or ideology.

With this has also come the clear realization that the problems facing the Muslim world today are, very logically and directly, the result of Muslims falling away from Islam and that they can be solved only by a sincere and whole-hearted return to it; among the social, political and economic principles of Islam, principles which are compatible not with the present savage, opportunistic dog-eat-dog ethics of self-interest but with the highest and noblest values of human civilization, are to be found solutions for its complex ailments. Of all the trends evident in the Muslim world today—materialsim, nationalism, socialism, Communism and Islam—only Islam holds the certain promise, if applied with sincerity and intelligence, of bringing the peoples of this region, who have lived through so many serious upheavals both internal and external in recent years, into a state of stability and peace. And without the slightest doubt, it is only Islam that can contain the spreading menace of Communism in its dangerous accelerating attempts to claim portions of the Muslim world for its own, for unquestionably commitment to the Islamic beliefs and values constitutes the only sure defence of Muslim countries, in their present unstable condition, against it.

In a broader context than that of conditions in the Middle East today, we may remark that Communism, materialsim and all other ideologies which deny or give insignificant value to man's spiritual nature or concentrate on one aspect of his nature at the expense of the others must ultimately be viewed as the human being's futile attempts, by means of his very limited human perspective, to understand himself and find the right direction. Since early in man's career on this planet, various religions, philosophies, and systems of life and thought, including those which are dominant today, have crossed the stage of history and played their role. A look at the legacy of this history and at current trends in the world makes it clear that none of these has succeeded in resolving the essential conflicts and dilemmas within the human personality, for all of them have, in one form or another, either ignored vital aspects of man's relationship with Reality or given prominence to one aspect of life or of man's nature at the expense of others, creating frightening disharmonies and imbalances within human individuals and their societies which have, in the present era, come close to destroying humanity altogether.

In the midst of all this, Islam remains the one system the world has known which views man in a correct perspective within the context of total Reality and with a correct understanding of his true nature, providing a just balance between his material and spiritual aspects, between the human being's worldly aspirations and needs and his eternal Goal. It is the only system which submits man and his life in its entirety to the One Who gives him that life and Who alone can be worthy of his submission, liberating him from the darkness of enslavement to man-made values, systems and desires into the light of 'ubudiyat to Allah, his true Master, alone. The truth of this is being realised with compelling certainty by more and more people in the East—those who were born into "Muslim" families but who have now become conscious, steadfast Muslims by conviction and commitment—and by many in the West as well. The grandeur and nobility of Islam is no longer an unknown, hidden thing, kept from the knowledge of the peoples of the West by lack of contact, prejudice or cultural differences difficult to surmount. More and more are joining the fold of Islam each day, realising that it offers them that truth and that way of life for which they had been searching fruitlessly, perhaps for years, in other and often totally contradictory directions. To many, Islam is increasingly throught to be the wave of the future, the long-misplaced legacy of the whole of humanity, not merely of people in lands where Islam has long been established, from its Lord, the Allah of the heavens and the earth, which holds out the promise to mankind, if applied with dedication and sincerity, of setting its feet upon the path of stability and balance, and bringing about such a total transformation in man's individual and collective existence as no man-made system, no obedience to gods of man's own invention, can ever succeed in doing.

SECTION FOUR:

The Islamic Way of Life

THE PERFORMANCE OF THE ACTS OF WORSHIP

The first obligation of a Muslim, no matter where in the world he or she may happen to live, is to establish the Islamic worships on a regular basis in his or her household. This means to observe *salat* regularly five times a day at the proper times, as well as the obligatory congregational Friday prayer; to fast throughout the month of Ramadan together with observing other recommended devotional practices; to pay *zakat* once a year if one has savings or property on which *zakat* is to be assessed; and to perform the *hajj* once in a lifetime if one has the means for the journey and for the support of one's dependents, and there is safety of travel to and from Saudi Arabia.

Let us now proceed to see how Muslims go about performing these worships in practical terms. *Hajj* has not been included in the discussion since it is, as a rule, a once-in-a-lifetime experience which we have already covered in detail in the preceding section.

1. Salat

The practice of regular *salat* is the most fundamental requirement in Islam, without which a Muslim is not fulfilling even his most basic obligation to Allah and may well have lost the most important and precious thing in his life, his perspective and sense of relatedness to his Creator. The *salat* itself is prescribed in the Qur'an and the manner in which it is performed comes to us from the *Sunnah* of Prophet Muhammad (peace be on him). Hence all the Muslims of today, no matter where in the world they may be, perform their *salat* in just the same manner as did the Prophet of Islam some fourteen hundred years ago. Consequently a Muslim from America can go to Tunisia or Yugoslavia or Japan or India or Iraq or South Africa or the Philippines or China, join congregational *salat*, and without the least difficulty perform his worship just as he had been used to doing in America because everyone else will also be performing it in the same way.

Salat can be performed almost anywhere—in a mosque, a home, one's place of work, outdoors or in any other clean place—either individually or in congregation. Congregational *salat* (consisting of two or more worshippers, one of whom leads the prayer) is preferable to individual *salat* because of its obvious aspects of Brotherhood and solidarity. In the Muslim world mosques are the established places for congregational worship. Women, as well as men, may pray in mosques if they desire, but it is preferable and customary that they pray in the privacy of their homes, especially since leaving the home and children to go to the mosque five times a day is neither practical nor possible for most women; many mosques have separate sections for women in order that they may pray in complete privacy and so there may be no distraction due to physical mingling between men and women.

So great is the importance of *salat* in keeping the Muslim strong and steadfast in Islam that it is an obligation under all circumstances, even when one is ill, travelling, or in battle. However, certain concessions have been made for such situations. Thus, one who is ill and cannot perform *salat* in the usual manner may pray sitting in a chair or lying in bed, moving his hands (or if this is not possible only his eyes) to indicate the various motions. When one is travelling, he can shorten his *salat* and combine the second and third, and the fourth and fifth, prayers of the day so that he prays three times a day instead of five; he can, if necessary, pray while seated in his vehicle or mount, and similar concessions are made for soldiers in battle. If *salat* is not performed at the proper time for any reason, it is to be made up as soon as possible thereafter; it may not be missed altogether. The sole exception to this is women during menstruation and up to forty days following childbirth; these are excused from *salat* entirely for the duration of their condition for the reason that cleanliness (that is, the absence of bodily discharges) is a requisite for the performance of *salat*.

Salat is preceded by an ablution known as *wudu* during which the exposed parts of the body are washed; this brief preparation of the mind and body for the act of prayer is an essential requirement. If water is not available (during travel or under other unusual conditions) or if its use is likely to injure the worshipper (as in the case of serious illness or wounds), he may instead make a symbolic cleansing called *tayammum* without the use of water. The ablution may be maintained from one prayer to another if it is not broken by any bodily discharge, such as urination or defecation, passing gas, seminal discharge, vomiting, bleeding, etc. A full bath by means of running water (*ghusl*) is required after marital relations, seminal emission, and the termination of menstruation or post-partum bleeding.

The five prayers are observed during the following time periods·

(1)	Dawn (*Salat al-Fajr*):	from the first light of dawn until shortly before sunrise;
(2)	Noon (*Salat adh-Dhuhr*):	from just past high noon until mid-afternoon;
(3)	Afternoon (*Salat al-'Asr*):	from mid-afternoon until shortly before sunset;
(4)	Evening (*Salat al-Maghrib*):	from just past sunset until the last light fades;
(5)	Night (*Salat al-'Isha*):	from dark until shortly before dawn.

After performing ablution, the Muslim prepares for his *salat* by determining the direction of Makkah (the *qiblah*) and facing it. For the sake of cleanliness, since his forehead and clothing will touch the floor or ground during prayer, he removes his shoes (except on occasion while travelling) and spreads out some sort of a clean covering, often a small rug. Men may not pray in a garment which does not cover them, at minimum, from the navel to the knee, and women are required to be entirely covered with a loose, concealing garment which leaves only the face and hands exposed.

Salat consists of a combination of words and movements, performed in units known as *rak'ats*. The worshipper begins his *salat* by standing at attention, raising his hands to the side of his head and pronouncing the words "*Allahu Akbar*" (Allah is the Most Great). This utterance constitutes a declaration that he is now in the presence of Allah and consecrated to His worship, and this phrase is repeated again and again with each change of posture throughout the prayer.

In the first *rak'at* the worshipper, standing quietly at attention, recites the opening verses of the Qur'an. *Surat al-Fateha*, followed by another Qur'anic passage of his choosing. After this he bows with his hands on his knees, as one who is ready to receive his Master's orders, while he whispers words of glorification of Allah. After briefly standing erect for a moment, he prostrates himself on the floor or ground in a gesture of total submission and humility before Allah, while he silently repeats words of glorification. This is followed by the second *rak'at*, performed in an identical manner. After every two *rak'ats* the worshipper sits briefly, praising Allah, invoking His peace on the Prophet, on himself and on all righteous people, and repeating the declaration of faith. The remaining *rak'ats* are identical except that they contain only one recitation from the Qur'an (that of the opening verses, *Surat al-Fateha*) instead of two. The final *rak'at* is followed by the same prayer said in a sitting posture, together with a supplication for Allah's blessings on the Prophet and his people, and then the *salat* finishes with the greeting of peace. "*Assalamu alaikum wa rahmatAllah*" (Peace be on you, and Allah's mercy). The worshipper may then remain sitting to offer his own personal supplications and glorification of Allah, either using the prayers of the Prophet or his own words and language.

A fixed number of *rak'ats* in each prayer are *Fard* (obligatory), while others are *sunnah* (that is, following the Prophet's practice and recommended but not obligatory). Thus, while it is permissible to pray only a minimum number of *rak'ats*, it is preferable to add to them the number of additional *rak'ats* which the Prophet used to pray and recommended, and if one wishes he may offer still additional *rak'ats*, again in keeping with the Prophet's own practice.

Congregational prayers are performed in just the same sequence and detail. In Muslim countries congregational prayers are observed

five times a day in every mosque, the time of the prayer announced
by the call to prayer (*adhan*) broadcast from the mosque, usually
via microphone. *Imams* (leaders of the *salat*), whose salary is paid
by the government, are appointed in many mosques; otherwise the
worshippers select a man of learning and piety from among their
number each time they gather to pray. The *imam* stands in front of
the congregation, the worshippers lined up in straight, orderly
rows, shoulder to shoulder, and leads them in worship; they follow
his movements in unison and absolute discipline, expressive of the
unity of Muslims as one Brotherhood submitting to the One Allah,
following one Prophet, and obedient to the leadership of a single
imam appointed from among them.

Islam also establishes a weekly congregational worship on
Friday (*Salat al-Jum'ah*), which is observed around noon in the
major mosques of a city, taking the place of the noon prayer for
those who attend it. This Friday worship is obligatory for Muslim
men to the extent that if one misses it for three consecutive Fridays
without a valid reason, he is considered to be out of Islam. While
the Friday worship is not obligatory for women, they may attend
it if they wish and find it convenient; otherwise they pray the noon
prayer at home as usual. The Friday worship consists of a sermon
concerning any matter related to Islam or the life of Muslims,
followed by two *rak'ats* of *salat*. The function of the sermon is to
educate Muslims in matters pertaining to their faith, recall them to
the observance of its teachings, and inform them of current events
of mutual concern. Although in most Muslim countries Friday is a
holiday rather than Sunday, Friday has not been prescribed as a
day of rest but rather of obligatory worship, and work and business
transactions are permitted as usual before and after the time of the
Friday prayer.

There are a number of other forms of non-regular *salat* which
Muslims perform on various occasions. The more common ones
are the nightly, *taraweeh* prayers during Ramadan; funeral *salat*,
always performed in congregation; the *salats* of the two festivals
or 'Eids; *tahajjud*, the *salat* offered during the last one-third of the
night, which is especially dear to those Muslims who want to
increase in nearness to Allah by performing additional devotions;

and *istikhara*, a *salat* consisting of two *rak'ats* followed by an appropriate supplication, to be performed when one is faced with a difficult decision about which he seeks guidance from Allah.

The Muslim child who is born into a household where *salat* is a natural part of the daily routine becomes accustomed to it from an early age. He sees his parents and others praying and joins in occasionally in his baby's fashion when he is still a toddler. Because *salat* is to have pleasurable associations in a child's mind Muslim children are permitted to move among the worshippers without hindrance, following the example of the Prophet (peace be on him) who used to hold his grandsons on his shoulders while he prayed. A very young child can learn passages from the Qur'an in Arabic just as easily as he might memorise nursery rhymes, even if Arabic is not his native language and as soon as he is old enough he can learn their meanings as well. By the time they are seven years old, children are supposed to be praying all the prayers, even though they may have to be reminded again and again, and by the age of ten *salat* five times a day becomes obligatory. Thus the Muslim child grows into the regular performance of *salat* easily and naturally, step by step, as the means by which he expresses his deep love and thankfulness to Allah, not only in words but with his entire being.

Salat is the central point of the Muslim's existence, without which he would not be able to maintain a strong and vital link with his Lord or continue his unremitting inner struggle against temptation and wrong-doing. Thus, no matter where on earth he may be, it is at once his duty and a necessity of his being to maintain *salat* faithfully and, whenever possible, in the company of his fellow-Muslims. Hence, while many Muslims living in the Western world may not have access to mosques, in many communities congregational prayers, especially that of Friday, are observed regularly in some designated place such as a university facility, an Islamic centre, or someone's home.

2. Sawm

The month of Ramadan is a period of special religious significance and activity during which Muslims fast each day as a means of learning discipline, self-restraint and flexibility. On the material level, the fasting of Ramadan involves total abstinence from all food, drink, tobacco and marital intercourse during the daylight hours, and on the behavioural level, abstinence from falsehood, speaking ill of others, quarreling or engaging in angry talk, discussion of disreputable matters, and wrong behaviour of any sort.

In addition to this, throughout Ramadan especially intensive devotional activities are carried on, both individually and collectively. It is *sunnah* to complete the reading or recitation of the Holy Qur'an during this month. *Taraweeh salat* is performed every night after the final prayer of the day, either individually or in congregation; it consists of between eight and twenty *raka'ats*, performed in sets of two *rak'ats* each. During the final ten days of Ramadan, many Muslims throughout the world observe retreat in mosques, spending the time in prayer and reading the Qur'an, and during this period the Night of Power, which will be discussed in the next section, is also commemorated.

The keynote to all the observances of Ramadan is self-discipline and self-control. Although in some Muslim countries the work schedule is modified during this month, in many places Muslims must carry on with their work and other activities even though they may be hungry, thirsty and tired. Fasting is in no sense an excuse for neglect of work or obligations, idleness, irritability or outbursts of temper, but, on the contrary, should be a total inner state leading to patience and self-control.

Although fasting does not become obligatory on Muslim youngsters until they reach puberty, many children have had some practice at fasting long before they reach that age. A special atmosphere prevails in Muslim countries throughout Ramadan. As a rule, even those Muslims who do not observe *salat* or other Islamic obligations fast during this month, for fasting in Ramadan is a community-wide observance with social as well as spiritual aspects. In spite of the apparent hardship of fasting, Ramadan is a very enjoyable period, especially in the Muslim world, to which people look forward year after year. And when 'Eid al-Fitr, the Festival of Fast-Breaking, comes at the conclusion of the month, it is a wonderful and happy occasion for all Muslims, especially for the children.

Let us now take a look at the basic rules of fasting. Actually they are quite simple. First of all, everyday of Ramadan is a day of fasting.[1] And fasting is obligatory on all Muslims past puberty, with the following exceptions: sick person to whom fasting is likely to be injurious, persons who are travelling for whom fasting involves hardship, women during menstruation and up to forty days following childbirth, pregnant women and nursing mothers if fasting is likely to harm the mother or infant, the very old, and the insane. The latter two categories are permanently exempt from fasting, while the others are exempt only for the duration of their conditions and must make up the missed fasts at any time before the beginning of the next Ramadan if possible. If one has a permanent condition which makes fasting impossible or dangerous to health, he/she is permitted, instead, to give to a needy person a sum equivalent to one meal for each day he did not fast. If a Muslim is not fasting on any day of Ramadan for any of the above-mentioned reasons, he is not to eat or drink in front of others who are fasting out of courtesy and in order not to undermine them.

The period of fasting begins each morning of Ramadan about ten minutes before the first light of dawn becomes visible and lasts until sunset. A declaration of intention to fast — a silent statement in any words or language that one intends to fast today for the sake of Allah—must be made at some time before noon. It is *sunnah* to break the fast immediately after the sun has set, after which the evening prayer is performed, and to have a meal before dawn, at which time the next day's fast begins, and, of course, the *Fajr* prayer is observed at dawn as usual.

The practice of breaking the fast at sunset and getting up to eat before dawn is a special characteriztic of Islamic fasting which must be observed in all Islamic fasts without exception. In Islam

---

1   The penalty for deliberate failure to fast on any day of Ramadan except for the above valid reasons is fasting for sixty consecutive days for *every* day so missed, or, if one is unable to do this, to spend in Charity

contiuded next page

fasting is not an ascetic or self-mortifying practice but an act of self-discipline and obedience to Allah, and obedience includes strictly carrying out His order to begin fasting before dawn and break the fast exactly at sunset. Voluntary fasting outside Ramadan follows the same rules as the fasting of Ramadan. However, it should not be continuous, day-after-day fasting, apart from a few specific days during the year on which the Prophet himself (peace be on him) practiced fasting and recommended it. Again, although marital intercourse is prohibited during the hours of fasting, it is permissible during the night hours, once more making it clear that this refraining from meeting otherwise lawful needs during the daylight hours is intended as a means of self-discipline, not as an ascetic practice, which Islam dislikes.

It should be noted that because Islam uses a lunar rather than a solar calendar, any given date falls twelve days earlier each year than in the preceeding one. Consequently Ramadan (and all other dates) rotates throughout the seasons, completing the cycle of twelve months in about thirty-three years. Hence Ramadan sometimes falls in summer, sometimes in winter, and sometimes in between in the various parts of the world; people living in every clime experience it, therefore, during all the seasons. Fasting is naturally quite easy during the short days of winter, but can be extremely taxing in the heat of tropical summers. Under such conditions the fasting Muslim learns that food and drink are indeed precious gifts from his Lord, to be accepted with thankfulness and not taken for granted. He also learns to feel with the poor who frequently experience the same state of hunger he is tasting during this month, and thus his hands are especially open in Charity during Ramadan.

Although Muslims living in the West can as a rule carry out all their religious obligations during Ramadan without difficulty, they invariably miss the special atmosphere and activities which are common in the Muslim world during this month. Hence they often

---

Contiuted : an amount equivalent to feeding sixty persons for each missed day. The same very stringent penalty applies for any day on which one interrupts his fast intentionally without a valid reason. However, if one eats or drinks unintentionally, forgetting that he is fasting, there is no penalty since the mistake was not deliberate.

try to compensate for the lack of these by inviting other Muslims for *iftar* (the evening meal) and by community-wide observances such as frequent *iftar* gatherings as well as congregational *taraweeh* prayers.

3. Zakat

In practical terms, *zakat* is the sum of money which is to be paid on various categories of property, notably savings and investments, produce, inventory of goods, salable crops and cattle, which is to be used to assist the poor of the community, or for the welfare of Muslims and the propagation of Islam. *Zakat* is usually calculated at 2-1/2 percent, although there is some difference in the amounts due on various categories of "*zakat*-able" property. *Zakat* is assessed on money or possessions only after a year has passed since its accumulation, and it is calculated and paid once a year according to well-established rules.

Since it is the duty of the Muslim state to collect and distribute *zakat*, what do Muslims living in non-Muslim countries do with their *zakat* payments? There are a number of alternatives. *Zakat* can be paid directly, in such a way that it does not hurt feelings, to needy, deserving Muslims in one's own community; it can be sent to Islamic organizations or centres in one's country of residence to be distributed at their discretion; or it can be sent to individuals or organizations in the Muslim world for distribution.

ISLAMIC FESTIVALS AND OBSERVANCES

The pre-Islamic Arabs of Makkah observed numerous festivals which revolved around their polytheistic religion. After the advent of Islam, the Holy Prophet (peace be on him) abolished all these. In their place Muslims were given two major festivals, 'Eid al-Fitr and 'Eid al-Adha, the celebration of which, with the worship of Allah and with joy and happiness, is a religious obligation for Muslims. We will discuss these in more detail presently.

In addition to these two festivals, as we have already mentioned, Muslims observe the Night of Power (Lailat al-Qadr), the night on which the first revelation of the Holy Qur'an came to Prophet Muhammad (may Allah's peace and blessings be on him). Although its exact date is not known with certainty, it falls during one of the odd-numbered nights during the last ten days of Ramadan. On this night, according to the Prophet's *Hadith*, the doors of Allah's mercy and forgiveness are open to all who call upon Him. The night during which it is commemorated, usually the night preceding the twenty seventh day of Ramadan, is observed by devout Muslims by the performance of *taraweeh salat*, night-long devotions, recitations of the Qur'an and acts of Charity.

The first day of the month of Muharram is the first day of the Islamic year. It marks the date of the Prophet's migration *(hijrah)* from Makkah to Madinah, which constitutes the most important date for Islam because it signalized the real beginning of the Islamic community and system. In Makkah the Muslims had been cruelly persecuted, unable either to preach or to practice Islam openly. After the Prophet and his Makkan companions migrated to Madinah, joining themselves with the Medinite Muslims to form a single united community, they were able to establish an Islamic society and state practicing Islam fully and completely, with the Prophet (peace be on him) as their leader, spiritual guide and head of state. This is why 1st Muharram rather than the Prophet's birthday or the Night of Power constitutes the Islamic New Year.

Some Muslims also celebrate the birthdate of the Prophet (peace be on him); however, this observance is not based either on the Qur'an, the Prophet's *Sunnah* or the practice of his companions. Because Islam is not a religion centring on any human being,[1] the celebration of the Prophet's birthday is not a part of the religion but is a purely traditional observance, which is marked by gatherings or radio and television programes to recall the Prophet's life and mission, calling on Muslims to renew their commitment to follow his example.

---

1. This is why Muslims—that is, "those who submit" to Allah—strongly object to being called Muhammedans, i.e. followers of the man Muhammad.

We now turn our attention to the two major Islamic festivals or 'Eids.

1. 'Eid al-Fitr (the Festival of Fast-Breaking)

'Eid al-Fitr, the festival which marks the end of Ramadan, occurs on 1 shawwal, the first day of the following month, and its celebration extends over a period of three days. This occasion is a time of great joy and thankfulness for Muslims because they have completed their obligation of fasting, a month-long discipline of the body and appetites, and it is an occasion for celebration. The festival is characterized by a special *salat*, visiting and exchanging greetings and good wishes, and it is a time of special happiness for the children.

Before the time of the 'Eid *salat*, which is held in the morning usually shortly after sunrise, a special obligatory Charity must be given. This is a specified amount of grain or other foodstuff, or alternatively a sum of money equivalent to the cost of one meal, to be given on behalf of every member of one's family to needy Muslims either directly or through some Islamic organization.

The 'Eid prayer is a special, additional congregational prayer which is *sunnah* (practiced and recommended by the Prophet) rather than *fard* (obligatory). Traditionally in Muslim countries every able-bodied male attends; the Prophet also urged that all women should be present even if they were not able to pray due to their monthly indisposition. This prayer is held either in the largest mosques of a city or in an open area where many thousands of people can gather. It consists of two *rak'ats* with additional recitations of *"Allahu Akbar,"* followed by a sermon appropriate to the occasion.

Traditionally both the 'Eids are occasions for exchanging visits with relatives and friends throughout the entire period of observance of each festival. Gifts (usually of money or new clothes) are given to children, who delight in wearing their beautiful new things for the occasion, and special sweets or other foods are served to guests. Throughout the Muslim world, the atmosphere during the days of the 'Eids is distinctly special, combining social with spiritual aspects in a way which brings joy and pleasure to people of all ages and walks of life.

2. 'Eid al-Adha (the Festival of Sacrifice)

This is the greater of the two major festivals, the period of its celebration extending over four days. This festival marks the annual completion of the *hajj*. It falls on the tenth of the month of Dhul-Hijjah approximately two-and-a-half months after 'Eid al-Fitr, rotating clockwise around the year and occurring twelve days earlier annually, as do all dates.

At this time, those who have gone to *hajj* are completing their observances in Mina with the slaughter of an animal (although this is not a requirement for all pilgrims) and the termination of their state of *Ihram*. At the same time, as part of their celebration of 'Eid al-Adha, countless Muslims throughout the world are sacrificing animals (this is *sunnah* rather than obligatory) in commemoration of Prophet Abraham's readiness to sacrifice his son, Ismaeel commanded by Allah, and Ismaeel's willingly agreeing to be sacrificed, and Allah making a sheep to be sacrificed in place of Ishmaeel. The example of Prophets Abraham and Ishmaeel (peace be on them) is recalled on this occasion as a model of total obedience and surrender to Allah for Muslims of all times to follow.

Then what happens to the slaughtered animal? Its meat is divided into three equal portions—one for the use of the family, one to be given to neighbours and friends, and one to be given away to the poor, to be used as food; the portions which are distributed are given away as meat (not cooked or prepared). This giving of meat constitutes the special Charity of the 'Eid in the place of a monetary one, due to which 'Eid al-Adha is one time in the year—in many places perhaps the only time—when the poor may have meat to eat.

Apart from these differences, the other aspects of the observance of this 'Eid are identical to those of 'Eid al-Fitr.

How do Muslims living in the Western world celebrate these two festivals? 'Eid prayers are observed in every community where Muslims reside and gatherings to celebrate the occasion are common, for example, a community wide dinner followed by a programme with talks and suitable entertainment, a programme or gifts for the children, etc. Many Muslim children stay home from school to celebrate these festivals, and in some areas the 'Eids are recognized by school authorities as holidays for Muslim youngsters. Although it may take a special effort to make the 'Eids festive, especially for the children, in an environment in which Muslims are often a very small number, this is a religious obligation for Muslims as well as a social one wherever they may happen to reside.

FAMILY LIFE

Family life is one of the most important and emphasized areas in the Islamic system of life, and it is an aspect which remains very clear and strong among the vast majority of Muslims today. We will now have a look at the kinds of interrelationships Islam establishes between husband and wife, parents and children, and among other members of the family group.

1. Marriage and the Roles of Husband and Wife

Among Muslims the selection of a marriage partner is a very different process than in the Western world. Because Islam emphasizes chastity and modesty so strongly, there is very little contact between young men and young women in most parts of the Muslim world. Secondary schools are generally not co-educational and, except among the very westernized, boys and girls do not mix, date, or, in particular engage in pre-marital intimacy of any kind. And while love is certainly considered very important in the Muslim marriage, for Muslim couples love as a rule comes after rather than before the marriage.

The selection of a marriage partner is therefore generally (but not necessarily) made by the parents, especially in the case of a girl. The young people concerned can express a preference, can state what they want in a prospective partner, and can take an active role in the ultimate selection but ordinarily they do not go out and try to find a spouse on their own. Islamically, either the boy's or the girl's family may initiate a proposal but in practice it is customarily the boy who does the asking. This is done either through contact between his parents, other relatives or close friends with the parents of the girl; without the consent and approval of her father or guardian, who gives her away, marriage cannot take place. Depending on the traditions of the particular society in which they live, the prospective partners may or may not see each other before marriage, although Islam does give them this right. However, if they do meet at any time prior to marriage, this is always to be in the presence of other people since Islam forbids a Muslim man and woman who are not related to each other either by marriage or a *mahrem* relationship[1] to be alone with one another.

In Islam marriage is not a sacrament but rather a legal, binding contract between a man and a woman which establishes the licitness, permanence and responsibleness of their relationship, an acceptance of one another as spouses with a mutual commitment to live together according to the teachings of Islam. Both are to be mindful of their duty to Allah and their responsibilities to one another in all aspects of their interaction.

> "O mankind, be careful of your duty to your Lord, Who created you from a single soul and from it created its mate, and from the two of them spread abroad a multitude of men and women. Be careful of your duty to Allah in Whom you claim (your rights) of one another, and toward the wombs.[2] Verily, Allah is Watcher over you." (4:1)

As we have seen, Islam assigns the leadership of the family to men, for, in general they have been endowed with somewhat greater physical and emotional strength and endurance than women.

---

1. Near male blood relatives with whom Islam prohibits marriage, e.g., father, son, brother, grandfather, uncle, nephew; as well as father-in-law and brother through suckling the same nurse in infancy. The corresponding female relatives are *mahrems* to a man

2. That is, take care to maintain and strengthen the ties of blood relationship.

For this reason they have also been made responsible for supporting and maintaining women—not only their wives and daughters but also female relatives who may be in need of help and support.

> "Men are responsible for women because Allah has given the one more than the other, and because they spend of their property (for the support of women). Virtuous women are therefore obedient, guarding in their (husband's) absence that which Allah has guarded."[3]   (4:34)

The wife is her husband's companion and helpmate, who is, together with him, responsible for the affairs of the household, the physical and emotional well-being of its members, and the training of the children. She should obey her husband unless he asks her to disobey Allah in which case she must not obey him, and for his part he should be considerate and concerned for her welfare. As the above Qur'anic verse indicates, she is also responsible for the proper management of her husband's possessions and property, for the guarding of his honour, dignity and respectability, and for reserving her sexuality exclusively for the man she has married.

In Islam a woman, married or single, is seen as a person in her own right, not merely as an adjunct to her husband. Thus, for example she has the full right of ownership and disposal of her own property and earnings even after marriage, and when she marries she retains her own family name instead of taking that of her husband. The Western stereotype of the Muslim woman as a mere household drudge, preoccupied from morning to night with cooking, cleaning and looking after the children, with no spirituality, interests, personality or life of her own, who is debarred from contributing in a constructive manner to society, has no basis in the Islamic teachings.[4] For Islam regards men and women as completely equal in terms of accountability to Allah and in

---

3. Their husband's rights to sexual exclusiveness, his honour and his property.

4. The two women whom the Qur'an holds up as models of virtue (66:11-12) are the wife of the tyrannical Pharoah of Moses time, who, in spite of her husband's power and oppressive behaviour, kept herself aloof from all evil, taking refuge in Allah from his wickedness, and Mary the

Continued next page

possessing unique personalities of their own.[5] It prescribes for both the same religious obligations, apart from the concessions made for women's reproductive cycle, and makes conscious commitment to Islam, the doing of good, striving with all one's efforts in Allah's path, the development of spirituality and seeking

---

mother of Jusus, a pure and devout woman. Both of these were women of immense spirituality and nobility. Like them, the three greatest women of early Islamic times—Khadijah, the Prophet's first wife whom he loved so devotedly, 'Aisha, the quick-minded young wife of his later years, and Fatimah, his patient devout daughter—were examples of intelligence, deep spirituality and many other good qualities.

5   If men and women are held to be equal in Islam, why does it appear to favor men in such matters as inheritance (which stipulates that the share of the male is as a rule twice that of the female) and legal evidence (the testimony of two females being equal to that of one male), it may be asked? Although these two matters appear to concern the same issue, in fact they involve two totally unrelated situations. Let us examine them one by one.

As we have seen, in Islam the responsibility for the maintenance of women falls upon men. A woman's earnings, property or inheritance is unqualifiedly hers to keep and to use as she wishes; even if she has money, she is not obliged to use it for her own maintenance or to support her children or husband. It will thus be readily apparent that since man bears the economic burden of the support of women, it is only just that his share of inheritance should be more than that of a woman, who is free to spend her money in any way she pleases.

Concerning the question of the testimony of two women being equal to that of one man, so that "if (as the Qur'an says) one makes a mistake the other can remind her" (2: 282), this stipulation takes into account man's overall greater fitness for matters involving accuracy of memory, coolness of judgment, and the application of rational rather than emotional faculties. This applies to cases in which men are considered to be more knowledgeable and likely to be more fair and accurate witnesses than women; however, in cases in which women possess knowledge or judgment of a kind which is superior to that of men, the witness of one woman is held to be equal or even superior to that of one man. These provisions have been made to safeguard the rights of the accused, for in Islam an individual is innocent unless proved guilty and it is considered more desirable to withhold punishment from a guilty person than to erroneously punish someone who is innocent.

knowledge equally the duty of both men and women, as the following Qur'anic verses indicate:

> "And their Lord answered them: 'Verily, I will not allow the work of any worker, male or female, to be lost. You proceed from one another.'"   (3:195)

> "And whoever does good, whether male or female, and he (or she) is a Believer these will enter Paradise and they will not be wronged by so much as the groove of a date-stone."   (4:124)

> "And the Believers, men and women, are protecting friends to one another. They enjoin what is right and forbid what is wrong, they observe regular *salat* and pay *zakat*, and they obey Allah and His Messenger. As for these, Allah will have mercy on them. Verily, Allah is Mighty, Wise. Allah promises the Believers, men and women, gardens underneath which rivers flow, to abide therein—blessed dwellings in Gardens of Eden. And greater (than that), Allah's good pleasure: that is the supreme success."   (9:71:72)

At the same time, Islam recognizes that women have a more delicate, sensitive and emotional nature than men and men are asked to treat them in accordance with this nature. There are many beautiful *Hadiths* of the Prophet (peace be on him) which enjoin kindness and consideration for women and advise Muslims to treat their wives with respect, honour and that quality of tenderness which suits the delicacy of their feminine nature; the best men, he said, are those who are best to their wives.[6] Because the natures of the male and the female are not the same, each has been

---

6. At the same time Islam, which is for people of all levels and conditions, recognizes the fact that some women, those who are difficult, unresponsive or incapable of mature behaviour, do not always respond to good treatment. Hence men are permitted to show their displeasure to such recalcitrant wives by, first a verbal admonition, then leaving their beds, and finally a token beating. But this, by the Prophet's own order, is to be of such a mild nature that it does not hurt or inflict harm but rather serves to show a woman who cannot be reached by other means that the situation is now serious. In no case verbal or physical abuse which hurts, harms or humiliates one's wife is permitted by Islam.

entrusted with a particular role and function in society; these roles are complementary and each is equally basic and essential to the functicning of the society. Within this framework there is freedom for both men and women to pursue what is important to them and to contribute to society in keeping with their own individual skills and interests, provided their responsibilities for the home are not neglected and their work does not in any way jeopardize their dignity and modesty. Women must fill many essential positions in society which they can handle better or instead of men, for example, some branches of medicine, nursing, eduction, social work and other areas. In the Prophet's time we find women enduring persecution, exile and even martyrdom for the sake of their faith at the hands of the pagans together with men, and during battle carrying water to the wounded, tending the injured and on occasion participating in the fighting as well. We find them discussing and even disputing various matters with the Prophet himself, and on another occasion a woman standing up in the mosque to correct the Caliph 'Umar on a legal point. We find 'Aisha, the Prophet's widow, in later life an expert in Islamic jurisprudence, consulted by many eminent Muslims, while her sister 'Asma, as a young girl and again as an old woman of ninety, did great deeds of Courage and heroism.

Concerning the marriage relationship Allah says:

> "And among His signs is that He created mates from among yourselves that you may live in tranquility with them, and He has put love and mercy between your hearts."   (30:21)

> "It is He Who created you from a single soul, and from it created its mate that he might take rest in her..." (7:189)

The tone of marriage in Islam is thus one of mutual respect, kindness, love, companionship and harmonious interaction. In her husband, the wife has a friend and partner to share her life and concerns, to cherish and protect her, and to help her bear responsibilities which would be very difficult or impossible for her to handle alone, while a man has in his wife a companion and helper who can give him peace, comfort and repose in his struggle with the rough-and-tumble of the world's life. In the beautiful language of the Qur'an.

> "They (wives) are your garments and you (husbands) are
> their garments."   (2:187)

serving for one another the same function as a cherished piece of clothing: to be a comfort, a protection, a security, that which serves and beautifies and warms and enfolds and covers and conceals what is private from the eyes of the world.

Although for the sake of convenience women generally do the domestic work of the house, this is not required of them by Islam. A husband should help his wife with the household work following the example of the Prophet (peace be on him), who used to assist his wives, mend his own clothes and participate in manual work. And while the mother is generally the primary means of training the children, Islam neither expects nor wants her to carry out this extremely important task alone. It is the joint responsibility of husband and wife to bring up their children properly, and although the greater part of the daily work with the children generally falls to the share of the wife, the husband is the principal authority figure in the home who is responsible not only for the welfare but also for the behaviour of all members of the family. Together husband and wife must provide an Islamic atmosphere in their home and a consistent approach to training in which they reinforce and support one another.

The marriage relationship also involves another fundamental responsibility: the responsibility of both husband and wife to meet one another's sexual needs and at the same time not to seek elsewhere for the satisfaction of these needs. While marriage in Islam legitimises the fulfillment of an otherwise prohibited desire, it also requires that husband and wife reserve their sexuality exclusively for each other. There is to be no "playing around" in a Muslim marriage; adultery is, as we have seen, not only one of the most serious sins but also, in Islamic law, a heinous Crime. Moreover, the protection of women from anything which dishonours, degrades or in any way exploits their sexuality is considered extremely essential. Islam therefore lays down certain limits for both men and women so that sexual attraction and expression will be confined solely to the private relationship of husband and wife, and hence will not become a source of harm or disruption in the society. This topic will be discussed further under the heading of "Relations Between the Sexes."

Marriages among Muslims are, by and large, remarkably stable, especially in contrast to marriage in much of the Western world today. This is due to a number of factors. The first of these is that, unlike the Western marriage, in which premarital love and intimacy are considered indispensable, the basic ingredient of the Muslim marriage is a common set of values, principles and ways of living. Consequently a Muslim husband and wife, even if they come from different cultures and backgrounds, possess the same basic world view, frame of reference, and many similar attitudes and habits which serve to bind them together in a harmonious relationship. Second, even with all the problems and pressures existing today in Muslim societies, marital and family stability is encouraged and reinforced by various societal institutions. This is in marked contrast to many parts of the Western world in which the breakdown of marriages is assisted—one could even say made inevitable—by innumerable societal pressures which not only weaken the commitment of the partners to each other but also weaken the capacity of individuals to maintain a stable and permanent relationship with another human being. Third, Muslims are, as a rule, used to living with other people and are consequently skilled in adjusting themselves to various relationships; for this reason they tend in general to be somewhat tolerant and forbearing in their interaction with others, even when there are difference or frictions of one sort or another.

Another reason may be that Muslim men and women are generally quite accepting of their masculine and feminine roles. Consequently, because the division of roles and responsibilities between husband and wife is as a rule clearly defined and acknowledged, many problems and frictions are avoided. Again, Muslims are generally surrounded by a network of many relationships with relatives and friends. This gives each partner his or her own life apart from the spouse, with many other satisfying relationships, emotional outlets and sources of support. Hence neither husband nor wife is forced to depend on a single relationship for all their emotional satisfactions, thus putting an almost unsupportable burden on one's partner and untenable strains on the marriage, for the variety of rewarding interactions with others makes life tolerable even if there are frictions between the partners.

In summary, to the Muslim marriage is not seen as a Hollywood-style romance but as a flesh-and-blood relationship between two very human individuals. In such a relationship strains and problems sometimes do arise. When they do, they are dealt with within the marriage relationship, assisted by the cushioning effect of the society, rather than by breaking up the marriage and the family unit, which is in the long run more difficult and damaging than accommodating and showing tolerance and patience, except in extreme cases, in which divorce is not only desirable but essential. Because of all these built-in safeguards, therefore, marriage among Muslims is basically a stable and viable institution.

2. Parent-Child Relations

Among Muslims children are very much loved and wanted, a precious gift and trust from Allah. Although contraception is not prohibited, many couples have large families by choice because they genuinely love and want several children, and couples who are childless by choice are almost unheard of. Parenthood is regarded as desirable and rewarding, the fulfillment of a universal human urge which has its beginnings in a small child's instinctive love for babies and dolls. To the Muslim, his or her child is a precious treasure, a gift from Allah and the fondness of Muslims of all nationalities for children is well-known.

In particular the Muslim woman's role as mother is regarded as being of the highest importance, the most serious and challenging responsibility she could have. And the maternal role is not only rewarding enough to stimulate and give her great satisfaction, but it also provides her with status and position in the community. Muslim women as a rule possess a deep certainty that this role has been entrusted to them because of their innate fitness and capacity for the most important of all tasks: the shaping of the future generation of humanity. Islam acknowledges the immensity of the debt which an individual owes to his parents, and especially to his mother, his first school in life, in many moving Qur'anic verses and *Hadiths* such as the following:

> "And We have enjoined upon man concerning his parents: his mother carries him in weakness upon weakness, and his weaning is in two years. Therefore show gratitude to Me and to thy parents: unto Me is the journeying."
> (31:14, also 46:15)

> "Say: 'Come, I will recite to you what your Lord has made a sacred obligation for you: that you associate nothing with Him (as partner in his divinity) and that you do good to parents ...'"
> (6:151)

> A man came to the Prophet (peace be on him) and said, "Messenger of Allah, I desire to go on a military expedition and I have come to consult you." He asked him if he had a mother and when he replied that he had, he said, "Stay with her, for Paradise is at her feet."   *(Hadith)*

> Someone asked Allah's Messenger (peace be on him) to whom he should show kindness and he replied, "Your mother." He asked who came next and he replied, "Your mother." He asked who came next and he replied, "Your mother." He asked who came next and he replied, "Your father, then your relatives in order of relationship."
> *(Hadith)*

The birth of a child is an event of great joy and thanksgiving which is shared by relatives and friends. It is *Sunnah* to slaughter an animal when a baby is born and to feed friends and the poor with its meat as a token of thankfulness to Allah for the new family member. A male child must be circumcised at any time which is convenient (as must a convert to Islam) without any attendant ceremonies.

Parents and their children are generally very close emotionally and physically. Breast feeding is considered the proper way to nourish a baby and nursing may be continued, if desired, for as long as two years. Mothers (and fathers as well) often sleep with their children when they are young in order to give them better care and more security, recognizing that the young child needs his mother as he needs food and air, not less during the nighttime than in the day. Leaving young children with baby-sitters or in nursery schools is a practice which, until quite recently, was virtually unknown among Muslims. Children often accompany their parents, sharing in their experiences and pleasures and being part of their world, and if they must be left, as a rule they stay either with relatives, friends or trusted servants. Hence Muslim children generally grow up feeling very secure and loved, surrounded by a wide circle of family relationships within which they have a very secure place.

Training and guidance begin very early. Their goal is the moulding of the child into a sound Islamic personality, with a good character and morals, strong Islamic principles, sound Islamic knowledge , proper Islamic behaviour, and the equipment to handle the demands of life in a responsible and mature fashion. Such training does not consist merely of a set of directives but, far more importantly, the parents, living example of unfailing submission to Allah through a sincere and conscientious practice of the Islamic teachings. An essential part of this training, beginning very early in life, is obedience, respect and consideration for the parents themselves, as an embodiment of the well-known Muslim proverb. "The pleasure of Allah is the pleasure of the parents."

Islamic training aims, first, at giving the Muslim child a correct understanding of and relationship to Reality. He is taught very early that it does not consist merely of the material world which we observe and experience but of an unseen dimension as well, at the centre of which is Allah Most High. Allah's absolute power and sovereignty, man's total dependence on Him and his place in the scheme of things, the existence of Angels and also of Satan and his forces, are all an essential part of this Reality. A child is able to understand all this, as well as the purpose of his life, the certainty of death and of returning to Allah when he or others die, and the future Life in the Garden or the Fire, by the age of five or six, and it forms a vital part of his consciousness and comprehension of Reality as he grows up. At the same time, he is taught to love Allah, the Source of the innumerable blessings which fill his life, above everything, and that love and thankfulness to Him are best expressed in obedience to His commands. Meanwhile he learns about how Allah guides man through His messengers, and little by little the details of the guidance conveyed through Prophet Muhammad (peace be on him), whom he is taught to love above all other human beings, are imparted to him. Hence a sound conscience is developed early, and at a young age he is capable of being the watcher over his own actions.

As a result, when Muslim parents set guidelines for their child, he readily understands that the standards he is expected to follow are not just their own personal wishes but Allah's laws, to which the parents are subject just as much as he himself is. Conscientious Muslims naturally do their best to avoid behaviour, activities and companions which do not fit in with a pure Islamic life and associate with sound practicing Muslims as much as possible. They see to it that their child has proper instruction in the teachings of Islam and encourage him to fulfill his Islamic obligations; they place him (insofar as they have any choice in the matter) in a school situation which is good for his total Education, and are careful about whom he associates with and what he is permitted to do, while at the same time encouraging wholesome activities and interests. Islamic training is total training: training in Islamic concepts, principles, attitudes, values, morals, manners and behaviour. One reason why Muslims consider "family" so important, especially in selecting a spouse for their son or daughter, is because it is primarily the family which determines the sort of upbringing and breeding an individual will have; consequently a family of high standards and good repute can as a rule be depended upon to produce a young person—man or woman—of high quality.

As mentioned earlier, Muslim youngsters are considered by Islam as accountable to Allah for their own actions by the time they attain puberty. Therefore, at an age when in Western societies many young people are preoccupied with having a good time, personal appearance, sex, drugs or drink, conscious Muslim young people are already highly responsible, fearing Allah in all they do and trying their best to stay away from what they know to be harmful and prohibited. By their middle 'teens, a boy is well-aware of his future role as the man of his household and is mentally preparing himself for it little by little, although he may not marry

for several years, while a girl is readying herself for her future role
as a wife, mother and homemaker, even though she may be
continuing her studies for some time before she marries.

Today, when life in virtually every part of the world is confused
by the pull of conflicting values and societal pressures, the
conscientious Muslim youngster growing up in the Muslim world
faces many challenges and problems. Many—perhaps most—of
the young people around him are very far from Islam, often trying
to lead him toward various things he knows are forbidden or not
in keeping with his Islamic commitment; members of his own
family may also be very far from Islam and may resent and attack
his allegiance to it. And for a Muslim youngster growing up in
America or other countries of the West, especially in the case of
a girl, the situation is likely to be even more difficult. Throughout
this time of great stress, the parents are the greatest source of
support, understanding and guidance to Muslim young people,
offering them a firm yet attainable example of what they are
hoping and striving to become, and above all providing them with
the love and warmth which constitute the strongest defense against
the insecurity which prompts unhappy, unloved youngsters to
search for solutions to their inner problems through illicit sex,
alcohol, drugs or various deviant behaviours.

As the young adult Muslim man or woman gains experience
and knowledge of life, works at a job, marries and has children of
his or her own, the love and devotion between children and parents
is not in any way diminished. Now, through his own experiences,
he realises what they bore and sacrificed to bring him into the
world and to raise him, especially if he has been brought up as a
sound Muslim, and an adult-level sympathy, and understanding
now exists between them and him. And while there is a natural
branching-off when a young man forms his own home with his wife
or a girl goes to the home of her husband, the parents are not
replaced in their affection by the newly-formed relationship. For
a Muslim son or daughter of any age, love for parents is not a once-
a-year event to be announced with Mother's or Father's Day gifts
or cards but a continuous and permanent state lasting as long as
life itself endures. Although they may live in separate homes or

localities, or even at the opposite ends of the earth, parents and children remain part of a single family unit whose members are bound together by the strongest ties of duty and affection.

As the parents get older and their vitality diminishes, this is not seen as the signal to put them away somewhere where they will not be a nuisance or make demands. In Muslim countries there is virtually no such institution as an old-age home; the aged are cared for by their children as a matter of course or by other relatives if there are no children. A Muslim does not regard this as a burden, no matter how demanding their care may be, but as an Islamic obligation, a duty he owes them. In the beautiful language of the Qur'an:

> "Thy Lord has commanded that you worship none but Him and that you be kind to parents. If either or both of them reach old age with thee, do not say to them (so much as) 'Off!' nor chide them but address them in terms of honour, and out of kindness lower to them thy wing of humility and say, 'My Lord, have mercy on them as they cherished me in childhood,'"   (17:23-24)

To the Muslim, the idea of putting old people into "homes" which are in reality custodial institutions where they go to vegetate and die in loneliness and despair so that one does not have to be burdened with their care seems totally barbarous and inhuman, a selfish, ungrateful return for all they did for him when he was more helpless than they are now; he could never imagine that he would attain Paradise if he did this to them—or to his parents-in-law or other aged relatives as well, who are just like parents for him. It is simply obvious and understood that when parents reach this stage of life, it is their children's turn to take care of them.

A moving story is told about a Muslim who carried his old invalid mother in his arms for *tawaf* around the Ka'aba. "I know I am a very heavy burden for you, my son," she said, stroking his hair, "but do you know that your carrying me one circuit around the Ka'aba is not equivalent to one pain I had in giving you birth?" Thus the mutual love, compassion and sympathy between parents and children, lasts throughout life, and when death comes to the parents, even though they were old and infirm and could long ago have been expected to die at any time, they are deeply and poignantly mourned and missed, and their example serves to inspire their children and grandchildren in time to come. Indeed, the duty of their children does not end with the death of the parents, for they continue to mention them in their prayers and to make supplication for Allah's mercy on them until the end of their own lives.

3. Relations with Relatives

To a Muslim, close relations and kindness to other relatives is also very important. The grandparents are another mother and father who are to be treated just as one would treat his own parents, and aunts and uncles are regarded similarly. Sisters and brothers are usually very close, and their children are like one's own. Family ties are so close that it is not unusual for Muslims to assume responsibility for their younger brothers or sisters or for nieces and nephews or grandchildren if the need arises.[1]

If any of these relatives—for instance, a grandparent, an elderly aunt or uncle, a widowed, divorced or unmarried sister, or an orphan—are destitute, infirm or alone, these are as a rule provided for by some member of their family. In the Muslim world it is rare to find a person, man or woman, young or old, living by himself or herself, for people who are alone become the responsibility of one or another of their relatives, a member of their households, occupying a secure place in the family's life and in its regard rather than being left to struggle with the cares of life on their own.

Other forms of assistance to relatives when they need help are also very common. For example, if someone needs money, he does not go to a bank to get a loan at ten per cent interest; instead he borrows it from one of his relatives, who does not refuse as long as he has it to lend, even though he may have other uses or needs for it himself, and of course, accepting interest is not only absolutely prohibited to Muslims but also absolutely unthinkable from a

---

1. Islam does not include cousins within the circle of *mahram* relationships. Hence cousin marriage is permitted and is very common in the Muslim world.

purely human perspective. "Binding ties of relationship" is considered very important in Islam, while hostility or breaking relations with relatives is a very serious matter. Hence, if there are conflicts or breaches among members of a family for any reason, the Muslim has a duty to act as a mediator and try to bring them together.

RELATIONS BETWEEN THE SEXES

Certain elements are basic to human nature, and one of these is the sexual urge. Every society has certain patterns of sexual behaviour and these are never random. Invariably they reflect the society's value system and are a mirror of its basic attitudes toward human responsibility and accountability, the well-being of the family, and the purity and integrity of individuals and the society as a whole. The sexual mores of any society are therefore ultimately governed by its basic understanding of Reality, its fundamental attitudes concerning the origin and permanence of moral laws, and man's nature, role and responsibility in the world, as well as the nature and role of woman in society.

In a society which denies or which does not regulate its life by belief in Allah and obedience to His laws, man is regarded as a purely physical being who has a brief existence in this world. As there is nothing but the present life, it must be made the most of and enjoyed in every way possible before it ends, and no barriers or limits to enjoyment are acknowledged. Women and men are simply made to do what is "natural" without any significant moral or ethical considerations to hinder them.

In contrast, as we have seen, Islam emphatically rejects the notion that a human being is simply a physical or animal entity. Although it certainly does not deny that man has many needs and attributes which are common with animals, it does deny him the right to fulfill these needs in a purely animal fashion. Rather its aim is to regulate and channelize these animal aspects of human nature and to bring the whole of that nature, with its various facets and elements, into submission to Allah Most High.

As we saw earlier, the Islamic society is governed by a sense of both individual and collective responsibility to Allah Who has defined the limits for human behaviour. Accordingly, strong measures are taken to safeguard the purity and integrity of its individuals and institutions, especially the family. Again, Islam accords woman honour and dignity, and requires that she be treated with respect. Her sexuality may not be exploited in any way nor may she be treated as a "sex object": rather she is to be regarded and treated as a human individual whose sexuality does not enter into her relationship with any person other than her husband. Not only does he have the exclusive right of sexual access to his wife but also the right that her beauty and feminine attractions should not be shared with other men, and the same is true of the wife in relation to her husband. Based on these general guidelines, Islam has established certain principles to govern the interaction of the sexes and control sexual behaviour among Muslims.

The first of these principles is that free, casual social mixing between men and women is not permitted; in fact, mixing is discouraged unless it is for some serious, legitimate reason or purpose, not simply as a means of amusing oneself or enjoying the company of the opposite sex. For this reason, in many parts of the Muslim world, schools, colleges, hospitals, transportation facilities, etc., have separate sections for men and women. Homes are often constructed in such a way that men who visit the house do not come in contact with its women; male visitors are received by the men of the house and entertained in a guest room, while the women carry on their own activities in their informal home attire in other parts of the house without being seen by the visitors or inconvenienced in any way. Likewise, women also have their circle of female friends, and when these come to visit, they in turn do not mix with the men of the household.

The second principle is that when mixing does take place, both men and women are to exercise propriety in the way they speak, look and behave. Obviously a woman can be either business-like and direct, or she can let her sexuality into the picture in her interaction with men in innumerable implicit and overt ways. This Muslim women are not permitted to do. At the same time, men are expected to exercise the same restraint in behaviour, not to look deliberately and with interest at women's attractions, to be playful or "friendly" with them, or to have any physical contact with them whatsoever, but to keep the interaction strictly straight-forward and direct.

The third principle regulating the relations between the sexes in Islam is that a Muslim man and woman who are not related either by marriage or by a *mahrem* relationship are not permitted to be alone together. A well-known *Hadith* of the Prophet (peace be on him) states, "Whoever believes in Allah and the Last Day should not sit in privacy with a woman without a *mahrem* of hers being present, because Satan will be the third (among them)." How vividly this describes just what occurs when a man and woman are alone together, when the consciousness of their sexuality creeps in between them, affecting their relationship and making them feel for one another what should not be felt, disturbing their inner equilibrium and purity and leading them toward the possibility of sin. Thus, even when a Muslim man or woman meets with a prospective marriage partner, including after they are formally engaged, although they may see and talk with one another in the presence of *mahrem* relatives, Islam forbids their going out or staying alone with each other on the principle that if there is no occasion for temptation there will likewise be no occasion for wrongdoing.

The fourth principle is that the Muslim woman is required to conceal her attractions from men by a strictly modest, straight-forward type of attire. Within the close family circle, she is free to dress informally and to beautify herself; in fact, she is strongly encouraged to make herself attractive for her husband since her beauty is reserved for him. She is also free to do the same among other Muslim women if no man is present. But outside her home and at any time when she is in the presence of *non-mahrem* men, even within her home, she is required to wear a covering-type of dress which will make it clear to anyone who sees her that she is a chaste, modest and pure woman, and that she does not want her sexuality to enter into the interaction in the slightest degree.

A Muslim woman in this business-like, non-attracting kind of dress which brings out her femininity while concealing her sexuality, and with correspondingly straight-forward behaviour, automatically elicits and receives the respect of men just as nuns, whose habits are somewhat similar to the covering dress of Muslim women, have always been respected. This type of dress, which is known as *hijab* or *purdah*, is prescribed by a direct order in the Qur'an and is a characteriztic by which a conscientious Muslim woman is recognizable anywhere in the world. We will have more to say on this subject in the section on clothing.

It is within this context that the Islamic concept of womanhood may be understood most clearly. The respect and status which a Muslim woman enjoys are not tied up in any way with her physical attractiveness or social skills in relation to men; rather it is concealing and reserving her beauty and sexuality, her feminine charms and favours, exclusively for the man she has married which marks her as a virtuous woman and gains her respect. Indeed, Islam prescribes *hijab* not only to protect society from the disruption produced by uncontrolled expressions of sexual interest and in order to protect womans' dignity and honour, but also in order to neutralise her sexuality so that she can be a positive, constructive force in society rather than a harmful one. Due to this modest dress and the propriety of her manner and behaviour, men can regard and treat her as a person, not a sex object; that is, her value to the society has no relationship to her physical attractions but solely to her worth as a human being. Consequently, as a Muslims woman grows older she loses none of her value either in her own eyes or in the sight of society, for among Muslims a woman's worth, like a man's, increases with age due to her wisdom and experience instead of decreasing with her declining youthfulness and beauty. For the Muslim woman, her character and personal attainments, her modesty and dignity, her piety and intelligence, and her feminine role as wife and mother are the sources of status and respect within the community rather than her possessing sexual interest, attractiveness or easy sociability with men.

But lest it be thought that the responsibility for maintaining pure relations with the opposite sex rests with women alone, we have only to cite the following well-known Qur'anic verse:

"Tell the believing men to lower their gaze [1] and guard their sexuality; that is purer for them. Indeed, Allah is aware of what they do. And tell the believing women to lower their gaze and guard their sexuality ..." (24:30-31)

The Islamic teachings thus inculcate in men and women alike a strong sense of *haya*, that is, shyness, reserve and modesty in the presence of the opposite sex (and indeed, in relation to modesty of one's own sex as well), which acts as a very strong deterrent against indecency. Due to this, a conscious Muslim man avoids just as scrupulously as his Muslim sister anything which would lead him toward what is forbidden or would lower him in his own eyes or before his Lord; likewise his dress and manner demonstrate that he possesses self-respect and is free of indecent intentions and desires. [2] In short, chastity, modesty and purity are not merely external restraints imposed by religion or society but are rather inner qualities which devout Muslim men as well as women deeply cherish and desire to uphold.

It will be obvious from this that Muslims generally do not feel at ease with the current trends in Western society. Conscientious Muslims who come to visit or to live in Western countries are often deeply shocked by the general lack of shame and modesty, by the fact that illicit sex is no longer censured in the society as a whole, and they regard the open display of flesh and the overt sexual behaviour which they see all around them as animalistic and degrading. The fact that sexual undertones can be observed in innumerable aspects of the interaction between men and women in Western society—between a professor and his student, a doctor and his patient, or a boss and a secretary in an office, for example, and between neighbours, friends and even relatives—in the form of the off—color joke, the compliments, the back-patting, the constant undercurrent of sexually-tinged innuendo which one encounters on so many occasions is also very distressing to them.

---

1. Not to look very directly or with interest or sexual intent at the opposite s   .

2. Islam does not require men to wear a particular type of dress but it does require that their dress be modest. As we are all aware any dress can be worn either in a modest manner or in a manner which betrays other motives.

Among Muslims, apart from the very westernized and others, primarily young people, who have lost their sense of direction, such behaviour is very rare indeed; certainly the interaction of men and women who fear Allah and strictly observe His limits is completely free of these elements. The observing of the limits informs both the man and the woman that there is no place and no wish for anything to do with sex in their interaction; indeed, if there were such undertones it would be felt as a great threat as well as a gross insult, and would render further interaction prohibited and impossible. To a conscious Muslim man or woman, attention from any member of the opposite sex other than one's own spouse in the form of free talk, compliments, playfulness, suggestive comments, touching in any form (including handshaking and patting on the back), and anything else which has sexual undertones is insulting, degrading and very much disliked.

In summary, Islam regards the sexual urge as an extremely powerful element in human nature, one which clamours for free expression if given even slight encouragement. Without such guidelines and limits for governing it as we have just discussed, and without the certainty that such behaviour is forbidden and will be very severely punished in the Hereafter, it will naturally seek to express itself freely, as we see in Western societies. Recognizing the strength of this drive and the fact that it is always present in any situation where men and women interact freely with one another, are alone together, and where bodies are exposed, Islam does not permit any of these things; for it is obviously far more desirable and effective—as well as much more realistic—to prevent temptation than to expect people to resist it when circumstances impel them toward it.

Islam also insists on the right of an individual to have a spouse who belongs exclusively to him/her; that is, one whose body has not been tested and enjoyed by the eyes or the hands of others. It totally rejects the notion that what people feel for each other or the pleasure they drive from an act should be taken as the criteria of right and wrong, and that obedience to the unbridled demands of animal desires should be permitted to dominate the lives of human beings. The moral and spiritual harm done to individuals, and through them to their society when they disregard the vital need of the human personality for purity and integrity to follow blind physical desire, cannot be assessed by anyone but Allah, Who has so clearly and absolutely prohibited such acts, and Who has also informed us the awesome penalties which such prescribed deeds will incur in the Life-to-Come.

DAILY LIFE

As we pointed out earlier, in Islam the broad meaning of worship is not confined to so-called "religious" observances such as praying and fasting. Rather everything which people do in keeping with Allah's laws in order to satisfy their legitimate needs and those of their families or society is considered worship, broadening its definition to include all one does with the intention of pleasing Allah in any aspect of life. Without this overall intention of pleasing and obeying Allah, no deeds, no matter how "good" they may be in content or results, are acceptable to or will be rewarded by Allah, for they have been done for some motive other than obtaining His pleasure and hence the reward of them has been sought—and often found—elsewhere.

For the conscious Muslim, the Holy Qur'an and the *Sunnah* of the Prophet (peace be on him) are the guide in all aspects of existence. The Qur'an is a book of life which he opens several times daily, either the printed Book itself or that portion of it which he has committed to memory, turning to it again and again both during *salat* and at other times as well for guidance, understanding, support, comfort and the remembrance of Allah Most High. Similarly, the Prophet's *Sunnah* (his words and deeds) is a vital, living example which he tries his best to follow in all matters, small and great, knowing that no other pattern of conduct or life could be as worthy to be emulated as that of the noble, inspired Messenger of Allah (may His peace and blessings be on him).

With this in mind, we now turn our attention to the application of Islam to basic aspects of human life.

1. Work and Striving

Work and striving in the worldly realm are a very important part of the Muslim's practice of Islam. Since administering the affairs of the earth in the best possible manner in man's responsibility, managing its resources, developing science, industry, technology, human potential and abilities, and mastering the entire multitude of skills necessary for the effective and smooth running of society are a religious obligation. All this can only come about by the expenditure of sincere and dedicated effort. "The Qur'an is explicit in stating that Allah's help comes only to those who work and strive with commitment and sincerity":

> "And those who strive hard for Us, We will most certainly
> guide them in Our paths, for Verily Allah is with those
> who do right."   (29:69)

> "And we shall try you until We have known those among
> you who strive hard and who are patient, and until We test
> your record."   (47:31)

> "... That man has nothing but what he strives for, and that
> his striving will be seen, and that afterwards he will be
> repaid for it with the fullest repayment, and that to thy
> Lord is the goal."   (53:39-42)

Hence Islam respects honest effort and work of any kind, and does not consider any necessary or useful endeavour as degrading. If a need for some service or skill is felt by the Muslim community, whether it be for a high-level scientist or someone to collect the garbage, it becomes an obligation on some members of the society to master whatever knowledge or skills may be necessary and to engage in this work. And whatever is done should be done in the best and most excellent manner possible, in keeping with the Prophet's saying, "Allah loves that when any of you does anything, he should do it in the best way." The only prohibited endeavours are those which are connected with prohibited activities, i.e., making a living by gambling, earning interest, magic or fortune-telling, pornography, prostitution or any other form of sexual contact or display, and by anything related to the production or consumption of alcohol, harmful drugs or pork. And while Islam does not prohibit women from working, they are not permitted to do so in situations where they come in casual contact with men, are exposed to temptations or degradation of any sort, or where their bodies become the focus of interest or their modesty is affected.

In the Islamic system of life, every member of the community must contribute whatever he or she is capable of for the good of society, whether it is a child or youth who is studying in order to master necessary knowledge or skills, a woman in her role as the manager of her household, or a man with whatever abilities, physical or intellectual, he may possess. Islam is not a system which permits praying or meditating all day long or living the life of an ascetic while making no effort either for oneself or for others. Once the Prophet (peace be on him) was told about a man who spent all his time in the mosque praying. He asked, "Then who feeds him?" "His brother," was the reply, "Then his brother is better than he," he said, underscoring the point that the religion of Islam does not consist merely of piety and devotional activities but also of hard work and reliance upon one's own efforts. Even the most pious and devout of the Prophet's companions, with the exception of a handful of men who devoted themselves exclusively to worship and the study of Islam, had an occupation or calling of some sort. Many of them were engaged in trade or business, as was the Prophet himself earlier in life. For example, Abu Bakr Siddiq and 'Uthman bin Affan, two of the Prophet's closest friends who became the first and third caliphs of Islam after his death, acquired considerable wealth through the prospering of their businesses, despite which they lived with the most extreme simplicity and austerity, and from time to time gave away virtually everything they possessed for the cause of Islam.

Thus, while Islam had made it the responsibility of Muslims to take care of people who for any reason are unable to meet their own needs through *zakat* and voluntary Charity, it certainly does not encourage living off handouts from any source. Again, although Muslims are not supposed to turn away anyone who asks, Begging, especially by one who is able to work, is considered degrading and harmful. The Prophet (peace be on him) said, "It is better for one of you to take his rope, bring a load of firewood on his back and

sell it, thereby preserving his self-respect, than that he should beg
from people whether they give him anything or refuse him." This
underlines the respectability of any type of useful work and the
undesirability of living by the labour of others or by Charity,
whether it comes from individuals, organizations or the government.
Islam is thus a realistic system for living which condemns idleness,
prohibits asceticism and discourages Begging, for it makes it clear
that a human being's dignity and sense of self-worth, as well as the
well-being of society, are intimately tied up with sincere and
honest effort, not merely of some but all of its members.

2. Knowledge

Islam's attitude toward the pursuit of knowledge and Education
is summarised in the following Qur'anic verses and *Hadiths* of the
Prophet (peace be on him):

> ".... And say (O Muhammad): `My Lord, increase me in
> knowledge.'"   (20:114)

> "Is one who worships devoutly during the hours of the
> night, prostrating himself or standing, who takes heed of
> the Hereafter and who places his hope in the mercy of his
> Lord (like one who does not)? Say: 'Are they equal, those
> who know and those who do not?' It is those who are
> embued with understanding who receive admonition."
>   (39:9)

> "Seeking knowledge is a duty on every Muslim man and
> woman."   *(Hadith)*

> "Seek knowledge even if you have to go to China."
>   *(Hadith)*

> The Prophet (peace be on him) prayed, "O my Lord, do
> not let the sun set on any day during which I did not
> increase in knowledge."   *(Hadith)*

> "No gift among all the gifts of a father to his child is
> better than Education."   *(Hadith)*

The most essential knowledge, which a Muslim should seek
before everything else is a correct understanding of Reality and the

precepts of Islam, for upon this knowledge all his life and deeds depend. However, secular knowledge is also of great importance and should not be neglected. These two branches of knowledge, of spiritual matters and of the world's life, should be studied and mastered side by side, each supplementing and complementing the other, as was done in earlier times in the Muslim world, so that there may be no schism or conflict between "sacred" and "secular" matters, between the realm of the world and spirit, either within the Muslim's personality and behaviour or within his society.

Knowledge is to be sought both for its own sake, for the love of learning, and for its applications. It is the duty of those who have knowledge to impart it to others. According to a *Hadith*, a Muslim who has gone out or is travelling in search of knowledge is "in the way of Allah until he returns."

There are, however, various types of knowledge inspired by Satan which Muslims are not permitted to learn or to engage in, such as magic and the black arts, fortune-telling, astrology, and anything related to immorality or wickedness. And while Muslims are assuredly permitted to acquire the knowledge of science, technology and the like from non-Muslim sources, they are not permitted to acquire together with this knowledge the values and behaviour of people or societies which are not ruled by a strict sense of accountability to Allah. Rather they are to subject whatever practical and scientific knowledge they acquire to the Islamic criteria and standards, to apply whatever is appropriate and beneficial toward the building of an Islamic society governed by Allah's laws in all aspects of life, and to leave alone whatever is not appropriate or useful.

3. Money and Possessions

Islam freely acknowledges the existence of man's attraction to the material sphere—his love of wealth and possessions, houses and lands, buying and selling and acquiring things. It does not prohibit any of these, but it does require that he keep a correct perspective concerning their relative importance so that the things of this life do not become the object of his existence or his goal. The Qur'an says:

"Alluring to men is the love of things they covet—
women, sons, hoarded treasures of gold and silver, highly-
bred horses, cattle and land. This is the provision of this
world's life. Yet with Allah is a better Abode." (3:14)

"And whatever things you have been given are but the
provision of this world's life and its adornment, and that
which is with Allah is better and more enduring. Have
you then no understanding?"   (28:60)

Accordingly, the Muslim is permitted to acquire wealth and
property and to enjoy the use of his possessions; however, this is
to be balanced with a sense of proportion and moderation. He must
not become so involved with these things or with any sorts of
worldly concerns that they interfere with his relationship with
Allah or cause him to lose sight of the purpose of his existence and
his ultimate destination. Moreover, the rights of Allah and of the
less fortunate on his wealth in the form of the obligatory *zakat* and
voluntary Charity are not to be forgotten. For all of an individual's
wealth and possessions are a gift and a trust from Allah, not his
by right or simply due to his own efforts or merits but to Allah's
beneficence. As such, they are to be spent not only for oneself and
one's family but also to help others who are in want or distress as
well. And whatever a Muslim spends from his means for those in
need or in the way of Allah is a "goodly loan" to Allah which He
will repay with great increase in the Hereafter. In passage after
passage the Qur'an speaks about giving and spending for others:

".... Those who go in awe for fear of their Lord, and those
who believe in their Lord's revelations, and those who do
not ascribe partners to their Lord, and those who give that
which they give with hearts afraid because they are about
to return to their Lord—these race (with one another) for
the good things, and they shall win them in the race."
                                                   (23:57:61)

"You will not attain righteousness until you spend out of
that which you love. And whatever you spend from (your)
possessions, indeed Allah is aware of it." (3:92)

"Those who spend their wealth by night and by day in
secret and in the open, their reward is from their Lord, and
no fear shall be on them nor shall they grieve." (2:274)

These Islamic teachings inculcate in Muslims a basic attitude of generosity and open-handedness due to which, as a rule, they spend freely for others and money never becomes an issue or object of discussion among them; it is simply to be used, for others as much as for oneself. After all, which of us can be said to own anything? Today I spend for you, and tomorrow or on some other occasion when the need arises or it is appropriate, you spend for me.

At the same time, Islam discourages wastefulness, indulgence in unreasonable luxuries, and spending for show or to impress others. Simplicity, contentment and thankfulness for whatever Allah has seen fit to bestow on one are important qualities, while pride in one's wealth, a sense of being above others who have less, greed or miserliness are very great sins. Money is of value only for what it can do, not for itself. It is therefore not to be hoarded or allowed to sit idle in the form of savings but is either to be spent for legitimate needs or to help others, or to be kept in circulation by appropriate and beneficial investment.

4. Food and Eating

Like the other good things of life, food and drink are not to be taken for granted. Rather they are to be accepted with thankfulness as the bounty of Allah and to be used wisely and for the maintenance of health. The Prophet (peace be on him) said that the Muslims are those who do not eat unless they are hungry and when they eat they do not fill themselves. Again, he said that one-third of the stomach is for food, one-third for liquids, and one-third for air, all pointing to moderation in food habits and to the desirability of eating to maintain physical well-being rather than simply for enjoyment, although food is certainly meant to be enjoyed as well.

The Muslim pronounces the name of Allah ("*Bismillah ar-Rahman ar-Raheem*"-In the name of Allah, the Merciful, the Mercy-Giving) when he begins to eat or drink, just as when he begins any other undertaking, and ends his meal with brief words of thanksgiving to Allah. Muslims consider it a blessing to have guests to share their food, and they are renowned for their hospitality, which is at the same time an Islamic obligation. This comes from the deep conviction that it is Allah Who feeds all creatures, not this or that person; all will eat, both host and guest, whether by one person's means or another's. One person's food is sufficient for two, the Prophet (peace be on him) said, the food of two is sufficient for four and the food of four sufficient for eight; for where there is true brotherliness and goodwill, food can be stretched indefinitely so that all who are hungry can have a share. In the same way, one's house and the food in it do not belong exclusively to the host but also to the guest who shares it. Among Muslims it is customary to tell the visitor, in effect, "Brother or sister, this house is your house, so please be completely at home and comfortable in it, and have whatever you like from it." However, the guest is also supposed to be considerate. His right to hospitality is for three days only, and whatever exceeds that is an act of generosity on the part of the host, not the visitor's right.

Islam regards wasting food as a sin and an indication of contempt for Allah's precious gifts and bounties, which makes even such a seemingly small thing as throwing away a piece of bread or treading on crumbs an impious act. Consequently, in Muslim countries if leftover food is not stored, it is as a rule given to servants, to needy people or beggars, or to animals who also require food, in keeping with the Prophet's example, rather than being thrown away.

Which foods and drinks are permitted to Muslims and which are prohibited? As we saw earlier, in Islam the principle is that whatever is not specifically (or by analogy) prohibited is permissible; hence all foods and drinks are allowed except the following which are prohibited in the Qur'an: (1) anything which intoxicates or interferes with the clear functioning of the mind, in any quantity or form; (2) pork and its by-products in any form; (3) the flesh of animals which have died without being slaughtered and bled fully (with the exception of game animals), those which have been killed by a blow, by falling from a height or by being gored with horns; (4) blood; and (5) any food over which the name of a deity other than Allah has been invoked and the meat of an animal slaughtered in the name of anyone other than Allah. To this list may be added, by analogy, birds of prey, animals with claws and fangs, rodents and reptiles, and insects with the exception of locusts. All seafoods are permissible; nothing is specified about the manner of killing them and the restrictions applying to meat do not apply to them.

The manner of slaughtering an animal prescribed by Islam is to slit its throat in a swift and merciful manner, saying *"Bismillah, Allahu Akbar"* (In the name of Allah, Allah is the Most Great) in acknowledgement that the life of this creature of Allah is taken by His permission to meet one's lawful need for food; the animal is then bled completely. Consequently many Muslims living in non-Muslim countries where Allah's name is not pronounced at the time of slaughter or where animals are slaughtered in a different manner consider commercial meat to be unlawful to Muslims, and they either have access to a Muslim or a kosher meat service, slaughter their own animals from time to time, or do without meat. Another opinion holds that since the Qur'an is quite explicit in stating that the food of Christians and Jews is lawful for Muslims, Muslims who live in Christian countries may eat commercial meat (apart from pork), pronouncing Allah's name on it at the time of eating. Today Muslim butchers and meat services are becoming increasingly common in Western countries in order that Muslims may have meat slaughtered according to Islamic prescription.

For those who invite Muslims to eat in their homes, it may be useful to list here the principal food which conscientious Muslims avoid. These include alcohol, both as a beverage and in foods,[1] and pork and its by-products; these are, apart from meat, primarily its fat[2] and gelatin.[3] Conscientious Muslims living in the West, and even in Muslim countries into which packaged foods are imported

---

1. All alcoholic drinks, alcohol-containing flavours such as pure vanilla and other extracts, cider and cider and wine vinegars are to be avoided. This also constitutes a problem in regard to medicines and other items such as mouthwashes which contain alcohol.

   Lard and unspecified "animal fat" are to be avoided, since many commercial fats are mixtures of pork and other fats.

3. Unless it is kosher or of vegetable origin, gelatin is ordinarily made from animal hide trimmings, including those of swine. Gelatin is found in gelatin desserts and salads, marshmallows, some cream pies, cake fillings, candies, commercial yogurts and other foods.

from outside, must read the ingredients of all packages to avoid these substances, and they often experience problems eating in restaurants, air-planes, hospitals, schools, etc.

People often wonder why pork has been prohibited. It should be noted that it was prohibited to the Jews in the Law revealed to Moses, and Jusus and his disciples, as devout followers of this scripture, also strictly adhered to this prohibition. It was not until after Paul proclaimed the Mosaic Law to be abolished that Christians began to regard this and other provisions of that Law to have been set aside. As for its prohibition by Islam, the reason for it is not mentioned either in the Qur'an or the *Hadith*. However, the prohibition is very explicit:

> "Forbidden to you (as food) are carrion and blood and swine-flesh, and that which has been dedicated to any other than Allah, and the strangled, and the dead through beating, and the dead through falling from a height, and that which has been killed by (the goring of) horns, and that which has been devoured by wild beasts except that which you make lawful (by killing it while it is still alive), and that which has been immolated to idols...."
> (5:4 also 2:173, 6:145, 16:115)

This makes it very clear that in the knowledge of the Creator there is something exceedingly filthy and harmful in the flesh of swine which renders it totally unfit for human consumption, placing it among other things which no one would consider as clean food. In 6:145 the prohibition is reiterated, characterizing swine-flesh as something "that verily is foul...." This is quite understandable in view of the fact that pigs are the dirtiest of animals and that they feed upon every type of filth which in turn becomes part of every cell of their bodies; they are also the carriers of a dangerous disease, trichinosis. In any case, whether the reason for the prohibition is known or not known, most Muslims obey it faithfully, realising that not all animals—even domesticated ones—are suitable for food even though the flesh may be good-tasting and readily available, and that the All-Wise, All-Knowing Creator is infinitely better aware of what is for the good of His creation than man, with his extremely limited perception and knowledge, ever can be.

5. Dress

Islam places great stress on cleanliness, hygiene and respect for the bodies Allah gave to human beings, for Allah "shaped you and made your shapes beautiful" (40:64, 64:3). As we have seen, cleanliness of body is a pre-requisite for the performance of *salat*, and in addition to this Islam insists on a very high standard of personal hygiene. There are many *Hadiths* in which the Prophet (peace be on him) enjoined on Muslims to be clean, neat, respectful of their bodies by taking care of them properly, and attentive to appearance, while discouraging unkemptness in dress and grooming, especially among those who are able to afford good clothes, for "Allah likes to see the signs of His bounty on His servants."

(Hadith)

It is a natural human desire to want to adorn oneself and one's surroundings with what is beautiful, one which Islam acknowledges and permits, with certain limitations. Accordingly, Muslims are permitted to beautify themselves with nice clothing, jewelry, perfume and the like, but for women these are to be worn only in the presence of their husbands, immediate family members or other Muslim women without, however, becoming very engrossed in or spending excessive amounts of time on these matters. What a Muslim woman wears among women or in her home when no non-*mahrem* men are present depends upon her taste and inclination in keeping with basic Islamic standards of modesty. For her husband alone she may make herself attractive in any way she likes since all her beauty is for his enjoyment.

We now return to the subject of *hijab*, the covering dress of Muslim women. Many people wonder why religion should have anything to say about dress as this appears to them to belong to the realm of personal taste. But as we have seen, Islam is not a system which concerns itself merely with the human individual's soul or inner dimension while ignoring his body, the external aspect. Rather it regards the human being as an indivisible whole and addresses itself to the totality of his life, requiring that the Muslim be a Muslim, reflecting the Islamic teachings, Allah's laws for mankind, with his entire being. This obviously includes appearance and dress, the keynote of which, as we have seen, is to be strict modesty in public.

Hence *hijab* is not an isolated aspect of the Muslim women's life but fits in with and reinforces the Islamic social system, and in particular the Islamic concept of womanhood. Just as Western forms of dress have developed from and fit the world-view, societal values and conception of womanhood of Western civilization, so does the dress of Muslim women emanate from and fit the Islamic value system and view of life. Yet *hijab* is not merely a kind of covering dress but, more importantly, something which the Muslim woman keeps about her soul and consciousness at all times to act as a barrier or curtain of *haya* between herself and the men with whom she comes in contact. As such, it is in fact the totality of her propriety and modesty in behaviour, manner, speech and appearance.

Then just what is the Islamic dress of women supposed to look like? The Qur'an enjoins:

> ".... And tell the believing women to lower their gaze and guard their sexuality, and to display of their adornment only what is apparent,[1] and to draw their head-coverings over their bosoms..."   (24:30),

and,

> "O Prophet, tell your wives and daughters and the believing women to draw their outer garments around them (when they go out or are among men). That is better, in order that they may be understood (to be Muslims) and not annoyed...."   (33:59)

The characteriztics of the Islamic dress are therefore laid down by the above verses and by a *Hadith* of the Prophet (peace be on him) which states that "Whenever a woman begins to menstruate, it is not right that anything should be seen except this and this"- and the Prophet pointed to his face and hands. Consequently, while Islam does not specify a particular style or form of dress, what is required is that a woman should be completely covered except for her hands and face (although the face may also be covered for

---

1   That is, the face and hands and whatever shows by accident, i.e. due to wind blowing the garments, etc.

greater modesty if desired), and that her dress should conceal her form, be loose and non-transparent, and not of a kind to attract attention by its beauty; moreover, cosmetics, perfume and jewelry (with the exception of what ordinarily shows such as a ring) are not to be worn in public. The dress of Muslim women should not be an imitation of the dress of men, and it should be such that the wearer can be clearly recognized as a Muslim.

Looking around the Muslim world, we find an amazing variety of garments which meet these requirements. The clothes of women differ from country to country, and in some countries even differ from region to region or among various groups within the same country. Muslim women are in no way constrained to wear a particular form of dress and are free to improve on or invent new types of dresses in keeping with the Islamic guidelines, as dictated by convenience or taste. However, whatever is worn should be a full and honest Islamic *hijab* which clearly reflects the wearer's Islamic identity, not an apologetic one or one which meets only part of the requirements. The Holy Prophet (peace be on him) very strongly condemned women who appear "naked while they are fully clothed."

This is the Islamic ideal. However, Western dress is now so common in many parts of the Muslim world that many Muslim women (and men as well) have never worn anything except Western clothes even in their own countries. Most are aware, to a greater or lesser extent, that Islam requires the wearing of *hijab* but they do not wear it for a variety of reasons, primarily because they are afraid of being considered "different" or "backward" if they do. Others wear *hijab*, but since they lack an adequate understanding of Islam as a total system of life, they regard it as more of a societal tradition than an Islamic obligation; when they make a trip outside or go to live in a Western country, they often remove their covering, not wanting to attract attention or appear different from others. Still other women—a large and rapidly-increasing number—wear *hijab* and maintain it wherever they may happen to go, convinced that what is required is modesty, whether it is "different" or not, and concerned with gaining the pleasure and approval of their Lord rather than of the people, with pride and confidence in their Islamic identity and attire. Consequently today in America and other countries of the West one can see many Muslim women, indigenous as well as foreign, clad in various forms of *hijab* as an integral expression of their faith.

People often suppose that it must be very difficult or impossible to move about freely or do work clad in such a dress.[2] This is not the case, as the vast numbers of Muslim women of all levels and walks of life who wear such clothing in virtually every country of the world can testify. Today numerous high school and university students, teachers, doctors and other women who hold important and responsible jobs in all areas are voluntarily adopting Islamic dress as being a vital expression of their Islamic identity. They lead very active and busy lives, *hijab* constituting no impediment to their work or freedom of movement. They do not regard wearing it as a hardship; on the contrary, they feel safe and protected because of it and would not exchange it for any other form of dress. For this modest attire protects the Muslim woman from the sexual interest and improper looks and behaviour of men; wearing it, she can move about it the world as necessity requires with dignity and a complete consciousness of her own propriety and modesty (it is obviously a bit difficult to feel really modest in clothing which was designed for anything except the purpose of modesty, no matter how modest one's intentions may be!) as well as of her clear Islamic identity, in obedience to her Lord's commands.[3]

Then what about the dress of Muslim men? Does Islam have

---

2. We often tend to forget that modern Western dress is a very new invention; as recently as seventy years ago, all Western women wore a dress similar to *hijab*. People who imagine that the Islamic dress of women is impractical and interferes with activity have lost sight of how active and hard-working women of other times, for example pioneer women, were in spite of their long, full dresses and various types of head-coverings.

3 Many people wonder about "the veil." The word "veil" has been used in the Western media to mean both a head-covering (which Islam requires) and the covering of the face. Veiling the face is common in many Muslim countries, either with a full covering or a parital one which leaves the eyes and forehead exposed. Today many sincere and

Continued next page

nothing to say concerning it? Yes, it does. First of all, modesty requires that the area between the navel and the knee not be exposed in front of anyone, including other males, excepting one's wife. The clothing of men should not be tight or sexually provocative, nor should it resemble the dress of women; in addition, it is not supposed to be an imitation of the dress of others so that Muslims may at all times retain their distinctive Islamic identity and character. The wearing of gold and silk, which are reserved for women, is not permitted to Muslim men. Although in many parts of the Muslim world Western dress is common among men, nevertheless there are many different and distinctive types of male as well as female dress. And while most Muslim men living in the West wear Western dress in public, in their homes and on various occasions they often wear their traditional dress, which has also been adopted by many Western converts to Islam.

HUMAN RELATIONSHIPS

The Muslim, acknowledging one Creator, sees humanity as one, all equally His creatures. For the Qur'an says:

"And among His signs is the creation of the heavens and the earth, and the variations in your languages and your colours. Indeed, in that are signs for those who know."

(30:22)

Contiuned : committed Muslim women veil their faces out of the conviction that Islam requires it or that it is best. Many others, however, veil their faces as a mere societal tradition rather than an Islamic requirement, and while the face may be nominally covered, the remaining requirement, of *hijab* are often neglected. Is veiling the face an Islamic requirement? The wives of the Prophet (peace be on him), who were to adhere to the strictest standards of purity as the "Mothers of the Believers." were required to veil their faces so that it would be impossible for anyone to think of them in sexual terms. This requirement was not extended to other women although some devout women during the Prophet's time did veil themselves in order to attain as high a standard of purity as possible. A small minority of Islamic scholars hold that covering the face is required, while the majority are of the opinion that it is not necessary or required by Islam, although in some circumstance it may be preferable.

"O mankind, We created you from a single male and
female, and made you into nations and tribes that you may
know each other. Verily, the most honoured of you before
Allah is the most righteous of you. And Allah is Knower,
Aware."   (49:13)

Thus to the Muslim, the colors, races and languages of human
beings—the obvious external difference within the family of man—
are signs of Allah's wondrous creativity, the Allah-ordained
diversity of mankind within its overall unity. Such outward differences
can never constitute a reason for either looking up to or despising
another individual, for the only criteria Islam acknowledges for
distinction or greatness among human beings are spiritual and
moral qualities such as the degree of *iman* and *taqwa*, the excellence
of a person's character, and his level of knowledge and practice of
Islam. Worldly considerations such as wealth, status, power,
family and Education do not count at all in the sight of Allah unless
an individual uses them to follow His guidance and seek His
pleasure.

Within the human family, those who hold the same view of
Reality and possess the same values will naturally feel the greatest
closeness and affinity to one another. Consequently the Muslim,
whether living in the Muslim world or anywhere else, will naturally
find his greatest source of support, affection and kindred feeling
among other Muslims. Regardless of their national origin, language
or cultural habits, the followers of Islam form one community.
Like the members of a single family, they care for one another's
needs and share good and bad times; they provide each other with
encouragement in living Islam and act as a deterrent in deviating
from it. The tone for the mutual relationship among Muslims is set
by many Qur'anic verses and *Hadiths:*

"And the Believers, men and women, are protecting
friends to one another. They enjoin what is right and
forbid what is wrong, they observe regular *salat* and pay
zakat, and they obey Allah and His Messenger. As for
these, Allah will have mercy on them. Verily, is Mighty,
Wise."   (9:71)

"It is He Who strengthened thee (the Prophet) with His

help and with the Believers, and He has put affection
between their hearts. If thou hadst spent all that is in the
earth, thou couldst not have produced that affection in
their hearts, but Allah has produced that affection between
them."   (8:62-63)

"The Believers are brothers. Then make peace between
your brothers and remain conscious of Allah that you may
obtain mercy."   (49:10)

"The Believers are like a single man; if his eye is affected
all of him is affected, and if his head is affected all of him
is affected."   *(Hadith)*

"The Believers are to one another like a building whose
parts support one another."   *(Hadith)*

"None of you has believed until he likes for his brother
what he likes for himself."   *(Hadith)*

Beyond this circle of his brothers and sisters-in-faith, to the
Muslim all human beings are brothers and sisters-in-humanity,
and the same obligation of kindness, fairness and consideration are
due to them all: For Islam does not permit discrimination in the
treatment of other human beings on the basis of religion or any
other criteria. Indeed, Islam's insistence on fairness and good
treatment to all human beings without differentiation is so strong
that it prohibits Muslims from behaving with cruelty or malice
even toward the people of the enemy in time of war. In particular,
it emphasizes neighbourliness and respect for the ties of relationship
with non-Muslims, following the example and injunctions of the
Prophet (peace be on him). The tone for the Muslim's relations
with other human beings regardless of their faith is set in the
following *Hadiths,* among many others:

"All creatures are Allah's children, and those dearest to
Allah are the ones who treat His children kindly." *(Hadith)*

"The Believer is not the one who eats his fill when his
neighbour beside him is hungry.'"   *(Hadith)*

"He from whose injurious conduct his neighbour is not
safe will not enter Paradise."   *(Hadith)*

Within this human family, Jews and Christians who share many beliefs and values with Muslims, constitute what Islam terms *Ahl al-Kitab*, that is, People of the Scripture, and hence Muslims have a special kind of relationship to them as fellow- "Scriptuaries." Islam permits Muslims to eat the food of Christians and Jews (except of course what is expressly forbidden, notably pork, which conscientious Jews avoid just as scrupulously as Muslims, and alcohol), and Muslim men are allowed to marry women of these faiths.

We will now take a closer look at some vital aspects of the relationship between Muslims, Jews and Christians in human terms and at the similarities and differences of Islam with their respective faiths.

1. Relations with Jews

Ahl al-Kitab denotes those people to whom Allah conveyed His guidance through a Divine Scripture or Book revealed to His prophets. In the case of Jews, this scripture is the *Taurat*, the revelation bestowed on Prophet Moses (Allah's peace and blessings be on him). However, this is not to be understood as the Torah (the first five books of the Old Testament) in its present form. Even a casual examination of these books makes it clear that, although they may originally have been based on a Divine Message, they were actually authored by human beings, since they contain innumerable marked inconsistencies, discrepancies and factual errors, as well as much subject matter which does not fit the criteria for a divinely-revealed scripture.[1] Moreover, these books

---

1. Only two examples of this may be mentioned here. One is the account of Creation (Genesis Chapter 1), in which Allah first creates light, and then the earth with its oceans and dry land, vegetation, etc., and after this, on the *third* day of creation. He creates the sun and moon. On the seventh day He is so weary from His labour that He must rest. Again, in Deuteronomy 34:5-7, in an account which is supposed to have been written by Moses himself, we read about the death and burial of Moses. The whole of the Old Testament is interspersed with such serious inconsistencies and inaccuracies that it is clear that it cannot be the original scripture revealed by Allah to Moses and the other prophets, although parts of it—what part is not clear, apart from, undoubtedly, the Ten Commandments—may have been preserved in it.

constitute primarily a religious, political and social history of the Children of Israel rather than a scripture conveying such clear spiritual and moral guidance, as well as accurate information concerning the true nature of Reality, as could have come only from the Lord of all creation.

Many elements, particularly the uncompromising stress on the Oneness of Allah and His guidance through the prophets, are common between Judaism and Islam, as one would naturally expect since both come from the same Divine Source. All the early prophets of the Old Testament are mentioned by name in the Qur'an and they are held in the greatest respect by Muslims. There are also many similarities in values, morals and living habits between the two faiths.

However, the problem of Israel has greatly damaged relations between Muslims and Jews, although the issue does not involve religious questions per se. It is natural and obvious that Muslims strongly deplore and oppose Zionist expansion, in the name of Judaism, into Muslim and Arab areas, for Israel has laid claim to territories where Muslims have lived for centuries, some parts of which are as sacred to the followers of Islam as they are to the followers of Judaism and Christianity, holding them to be an integral part of the "Jewish homeland," as well as essential to Israel's security.

Regarding the notion of a Jewish homeland, we read in the Jewish Torah that Allah said to Abraham (peace be on him):

> "And I will give to you and to your posterity after you the land in which you are a stranger, all the land of Canaan (Palestine) for an everlasting possession, and I will be their Allah."   (Genesis 17:8)

That the descendants of Abraham include Muslims as well as Jews is incontestable; therefore if the issue had really been related to and determined by Allah's promise referred to in this passage from the scripture of the Jews themselves, there would be no problem. As is well-known, Jews and Muslims had been living peacefully side by side for centuries in the land which Allah promised to the posterity of Abraham until the Muslims were dispossessed in recent times by the establishment of Israel. Hence this claim is simply a cover for naked aggression and the unconcealed desire for territorial expansion and conquest.

As we have seen, Islam does not permit Muslims to compromise with injustice and oppression. Since fighting for the basic human right to one's life, freedom, home and property is an Islamic obligation, they cannot remain passive while their people are killed or expelled from their homes and their lands are confiscated for no other cause than that they are wanted by someone else. The issue is therefore not in any sense one of religious disagreement— for none whatever exists in that respect—but rather a moral issue in which truth, justice and freedom from oppression are at stake.

2. Relations with Christians

Many important elements are common between Islam and Christianity. Muslims and Christians share many similar beliefs, values, moral injunctions and principles of behaviour. The fundamental difference between the two faiths concerns the nature and role of Jusus.

In Islam 'Isa Maseeh—Jusus the Messiah, Allah's peace and blessings be on him—is one of the greatest of the prophets whom Muslims hold in very deep love and respect. The Qur'an confirms that Jusus was born of a virgin mother (Maryam) through the same Power which brought Adam into being without a father, and that by Allah's permission during his prophethood he wrought many compelling miracles among his people. He was given the power to speak coherently in infancy, to heal the sick, to raise the dead, and to reach the hearts of men by the words which Allah revealed to him. Finally, when he was in danger of being killed by his own people, Allah raised him up to himself without his experiencing death (Holy Qur'an 4:157-158 and 3:55).[1] We cite here some passages from the Qur'an relating to Jesus' life and mission:

"Behold, the Angels said, 'O Mary! Lo, Allah gives thee

---

1   *The Gospel of Barnabas* (see the list of suggested books at the end of this volume) speaks eloquently of this matter.

glad tidings of a Word from Him, whose name is the Messiah Jusus, son of Mary, illustrious in the world and the Hereafter, and one of those brought near (unto Allah). He will speak to men in his cradle and in his manhood, and he will be of the righteous.' She said, 'My Lord! How can I have a child when no man has touched me?' He (the angel) said, 'Thus, Allah creates what He wills. If He decrees a thing, He says unto it only "Be" and it is. And He will teach him the Scripture and the wisdom, and the *Taurat* and the *Injeel*.[2] And He will make him a messenger to the Children of Israel, (saying): "Lo, I come to you with a sign from your Lord. Lo, I fashion for you out of clay the likeness of a bird, and I breathe into it and it is a bird by Allah's leave. I heal him who was born blind and the leper, and I raise the dead, by Allah's leave. And I announce to you what you eat and what you store up in your houses. Lo, herein verily is a sign for you, if you are indeed Believers. And (I come) confirming that which was before me of the *Taurat*, and to make lawful some of that which was forbidden to you. I come to you with a sign from your Lord, so keep your duty to Allah and obey me. Verily, Allah is my Lord and your Lord, so worship Him. That is a straight path."   (3:45-51)

"Verily, the likeness of Jusus with Allah is as the likeness of Adam. He created him of dust, then He said unto him 'Be' and he was."   (3:59)

".... And for their saying, 'We killed the Messiah Jusus, son of Mary, Allah's Messenger.' They did not kill him nor did they crucify him, but it appeared so to them; and indeed, those who disagree concerning it are in doubt about it. They have no knowledge concerning it except the pursuit of a conjecture; and assuredly they did not kill him. Nay, Allah raised him up unto Himself. And Allah is Mighty, Wise."   (4:157-158)

Then what about Christianity's claim that Jusus in the Son of Allah? In order to answer this question we must deal with two

---

2. The *Injeel* (Evangel or Good News) is the original scripture revealed to Jusus by Allah. This is not however, to be confused with the New Testament Gospels.

fundamental issues: (1) Did the Exalted Creator and Lord of the universe in fact have a Son, and (2) is it possible that Jusus himself could have claimed and actually did claim to be Allah's Son?

We note that although the Qur'an confirms that Jusus was born without the agency of a father, this simply means that Allah, Who establishes the regularity of functioning of natural phenomena which we understand as natural laws, is equally able to suspend them when it pleases Him—that is, He is able to create what He wills when, how and as He chooses. It does not make Jusus Allah's progeny or in any way a sharer in His Divine nature any more than it does Adam, who was also created without a father and likewise without a mother.

The Qur'an states emphatically in passage after passage that Jusus is not Allah's Son; that he never claimed to be Allah's Son or of Divine nature but rather charged his followers to worship Allah alone; and that the notion of the Most High Allah's having a Son is so totally degrading to and far removed from the exaltedness and transcendence of Allah's Divine nature that it actually constitutes an awesome piece of blasphemy. The Qur'an says concerning this:

> "And they say, 'The Merciful has taken unto Himself a Son. Assuredly you utter a disastrous thing, at which the heavens are almost torn and the earth is split asunder and the mountains fall into ruins because you ascribe to the Merciful a Son when it is not befitting for (the majesty) of the Merciful that He should take a Son. There is none in the heavens and the earth but comes to the Merciful as a slave."   (19:88-93)

For, the Creator and Sustainer of this infinitely complex and vast universe is far above anything we can conceive of, and the physical attributes and limitations of created beings can never be imagined to apply to Him. If Jusus were indeed Allah's Son, he would be a sharer in the Allahhead and of Divine nature himself, and in that case Allah would have simultaneously begotten, been begotten, been born, lived as a human being, and died. Such a notion does not merit any comment. It has much more in common with pagan mythologies, in which "gods" fathered semi-divine children by human women, than with a true religion coming from

Allah and based on the reality of the relationship between the Creator and the created. Hence the claim that Jusus is Allah's Son cannot be, by its very nature, other than a false one because it contradicts the very nature and attributes of the Creator Himself, bringing Him down to the level of the beings He has created. In the words of the Qur'an:

> "They say, 'Allah has begotten a Son.' Glory be on Him! Nay, to Him belongs all that is in the heavens and on earth. Everything renders worship to Him. To Him is due the primal origin of the heavens and the earth. When He decrees a matter, He (merely) says to it 'Be' and it is."
>
> (2:116-117)

We now turn to the second question: whether Jusus himself (peace be on him) could possibly have claimed to be Allah's Son. The answer is very obvious, that he could not and did not do so is clear from the nature of the Message he brought. Can it possibly make the slightest sense that Allah divides up His unique and indivisible nature between Himself and His Son, and that the Son commands people to worship him instead of his Father? This clearly means two gods rather than One Allah, the dividing of what is indivisible, and the splitting up of the power, authority and rule in the universe. Hence one is forced to conclude that the claim that Jusus is the Son of Allah could not possibly have been made by him but was made on his behalf and in his name without his knowledge and/or consent by some other person.

We cite here some Qur'anic passages concerning the nature of Jusus (peace be on him) and the Message he brought. These and many other references to these subjects recur over and over in many different parts of Qur'an.

> "O People of the Book! Do not exaggerate in your religion nor utter anything concerning Allah except the truth. Verily, the Messiah, Jusus the son of Mary was only a messenger of Allah and His Word which He conveyed unto Mary and a soul from Him. So believe in Allah and His messengers, and do not say 'Three' (the Trinity). Ceasel It is better for you! Allah is only One Allah. It is far removed from His transcendent majesty that He should

have a Son. His is all that is in the heavens and all that is
in the earth. And Allah is sufficient as a Protector. The
Messiah would never scorn to be a slave to Allah, nor
would the favoured Angels..."   (4:171-172)

"They indeed disbelieve who say, 'Lo, Allah is the Messiah,
the son of Mary.' Say: 'Who then could do anything
against Allah if He had willed to destroy the Messiah, the
son of Mary, and his mother and everyone on earth?'
Allah's is the sovereignty in the heavens and the earth and
all that is between them. He creates what He wills. And
Allah has power over all things.' "   (5:17/19)

"They indeed disbelieve who say, 'Lo, Allah is the Messiah,
the son of Mary.' The Messiah (himself) said: 'O Children
of Israel, worship Allah, my Lord and your Lord.' Verily,
whoever ascribes partners to Allah, Allah has forbidden
him the Garden. His abode is the Fire. And for the evil-
doers there will be no helpers. They indeed disbelieve
who say, 'Lo, Allah is the third of Three,' when there is
no deity except the One Allah. If they do not desist from
saying so, a painful punishment will fall on those of them
who disbelieve... The Messiah, the son of Mary, was no
more than a messenger, messengers (the like of whom)
had passed away before him, and his mother was a devout
woman, and they both ate food.³ See how We make clear
to them Our Signs, yet see how they are turned away."
                                                (5:75/78)

"And behold, Allah will say (on the Day of Judgment),
'O Jusus son of Mary! Didst thou say to people, "Take me
and my mother as deities besides Allah?" ' he will say,
'Glory be to Thee! It was not for me to say that for which
I had no right.... I said to them only what Thou didst
command me: "Worship Allah, my Lord and Your Lord.'"
                                                (5:119/120)

"Verily, he (Jusus) was nothing except a slave upon
whom We bestowed favor and made an example for the
Children of Israel.... And when Jusus came with clear

---

3. That is, they required sustenance for their existence like any other
   created beings, proving that they were of human, not Divine, nature.

proofs, he said, 'I have come to you with wisdom, and to make plain some of that concerning which you differ. So remain conscious of Allah and obey me. Verily, Allah is my Lord and your Lord. That is the straight path.'"

(43:59, 63-64)

"It is not for any human being to whom Allah has given the Book (a revealed scripture) and the wisdom and the prophethood that he should then say to people, 'Be slaves of me instead of Allah,' but rather, 'Be faithful servants of the Lord, for you have taught the Book and you have studied it earnestly.'"

(3:79)

" And behold, Jusus the son of Mary said, 'O Children of Israel! Lo, I am the Messenger of Allah to you, confirming that which was (revealed) before me in the *Taurat* and bringing good tidings of a messenger who comes after me whose name is Ahmad⁴...'"

(61:6)

If one drops any mention of "the Son of Allah" from the New Testament accounts of the life of Jusus (peace be on him), it becomes clear that he must in truth have been a prophet in the line of the other prophets raised among the Children of Israel who, like his predecessors, brought a revelation or scripture addressed to them by Allah. It is therefore impossible that this revelation could have been a new religion centring around Jusus himself; for one who was commissioned by Allah, the All-Knowing, to convey His guidance and call people to submit to Him, could never have claimed Sonship or divinity—something which no one possesses— or asked people to worship him instead of or in addition to Allah. Jusus himself strictly adhered to the Law brought by Moses (peace be on him), and his mission was to revive and confirm the Divine guidance which Moses and the prophets who followed had brought, not to establish a new religion. The scripture revealed through him

---

4. The Arabic names Ahmad and Muhammad are both derived from the same root letters *h—m—d* which mean "praise," and both have the smae meaning: the Praised One. Thus Prophet Muhammad is often referred to as Ahmad. It is also to be noted that the coming of Muhammad, the prophet raised from among "*the brethren*" of the Children of israel, may be what was prophesied in Deuteronomy 18:15, 18:19, and in Acts 3:22. See also *The Gospel of Barnabas.*

therefore addressed itself to the contemporary situation of the Children of Israel, insisting that the earlier scripture was binding upon them and must be followed, but with sincerity, inner piety and true Allah-consciousness rather than with empty ritual and insincere show of devoutness. Those whom Allah loves, Jusus taught, who will inherit His Kingdom, are not the inwardly-empty official men of religion but those who love Allah, obey His guidance with fear and awe in their hearts, and surrender themselves to Him. These are chiefly to be found among the ordinary people, often the simple and humble who are held to be of no account in the eyes of the world although their hearts are sincere and true to their Lord, instead of among the proud and status-conscious.

But if Jusus did not himself say that he was the Son of Allah and Savior of the world, how is it that the Gospels attribute such a claim to him? And how is it that all Christians since his time have believed this?

First of all, not all Christians, even at the present time, believe this. Some groups exist today which do not believe in his divinity, and in early times there were a number of sects, later pronounced to be heretical when it was "decided" that Jusus was of Divine nature, who differed on this matter, holding that Jusus was a human being and a prophet; among them were some which did not believe that Jusus was crucified but that another person very much resembling him was crucified in his stead.[5] Such sects were suppressed and almost entirely obliterated. Writes the American Muslim scholar Sulaiman Mufassir, *"It is significant that those doctrines which the Qur'an affirms can be easily proven to be part of the teachings of the early disciples, whereas those*

---

5. Sulaiman Mufassir, *Jusus in the Qur'an*, Muslim Students Association of U.S. and Canada, Plainfield, Indiana, p. 10. It may be mentioned that one of the characteriztics of a prophet accroding to Islamic belief is that because of his elevated station, Allah will not permit him to die in any loathsome or horrible manner, which includes such a degrading and agonizing death as crucifixion which was meted out in Jusus time to the commonest criminals. See also *Biblical Studies from a Muslim Perspective* by the same author, published by the Islamic Center, shington, D.C., p. 14.

doctrines which the Qur'an reject prove to be later Church additions, inspired by the philosophies and cults of pagan Greece and Rome" (italics Mufassir's).[6]

As to the claim attributed to Jusus (peace be on him) of being Allah's son, it must be remembered that the four New Testament Gospels, the books of Matthew, Mark, Luke and John, were written many years after Jesus' time. Biblical scholarship has established the fact that none of their authors was the immediate disciple of Jusus; moreover, they did not write in Jesus' own language, Aramaic, but in Greek. By the time they wrote their accounts of his life, a great many things about Jusus had been lost or forgotten and many more had been interpolated, and moreover Christianity was by then being moulded into a form which would appeal to Greeks and Romans rather than to Palestinian Jewry.

Now let us suppose that an individual of some note or fame were to live among us, carry on his work and depart or die. Can we suppose that an account of his life written initially as long as forty years after his death would be really accurate, especially if he had lived in a community in which writing detailed accounts concerning people was not common? And if he later grew into a public figure, something of a legend, we could be very certain that the narrative would in addition be considerably embellished by people's imaginations, and that at the same time a wealth of very important details would have been lost. The account would moreover be coloured by the understandings of the writers and would unquestionably reflect their own views and ideas concerning the person they were describing.

The accounts of the Four Gospels are analogous to such a situation. Jusus (Allah's peace and blessings be on him) most certainly did bring a divinely-revealed scripture. However, although it is obvious from their content that the Four Gospels do contain some parts of the message of submission and accountability which Jusus brought, these are simply biographical accounts of Jesus' life and mission by four different men, not the Divine revelation brought by Jusus itself. The greater part of the material contained

6   Ibid, p. 14.

in the Four Gospels does not meet the criteria discussed earlier by which a true revelation may be recognized, the first of which is that it should be transmitted word for word as received from Allah by the person to whom it was directly revealed, not through a second-or-fifth-hand source. Even the claim that the Gospels were written under Divine inspiration does not hold together since there are many inconsistencies and discrepancies among these four equally "inspired" accounts.

Without doubt, what Jusus (peace be on him) actually claimed was not that he was the Son of Allah (an incredible piece of blasphemy from the mouth of a devout and committed follower of the teachings of the prophets), but that he was the Messiah, a prophet in the line of the previous messengers of Allah, and that He received a Divine Scripture from Him. But it is apparent that the Message brought by Jusus, the message to the Children of Israel concerning their accountability to Allah and their obligation to follow the guidance revealed through Prophet Moses (peace be on him), was later changed, taken out of its pure monotheistic context, and made to conform to the pagan Hellenistic conceptions of the time; this was done to render it more attractive to the Greeks and Romans among whom it was being propagated, who would never have been impressed with the pure, simple message of submission to a non-corporeal, transcendent Deity which Jusus in fact proclaimed. That this Message was intended solely for the Jews and that it insisted on adherence to the Mosaic Law was completely lost sight of in this attempt to gain converts throughout the pagan Roman Empire.

The conclusion to be drawn from all this is that although in the Four Gospels of the New Testament we can find obvious traces of the Message which Jusus (peace be on him) brought in his emphasiz on man's accountability to Allah, the necessity of sincerity and obedience to Him, and the certainty of the Day of Judgment and the Hereafter, the claim attributed to Jusus of being the Son of Allah is so completely at variance not only with the Oneness and Uniqueness of Allah Most High but also with the remainder of the message of submission to Allah which Jusus brought, that it is impossible to regard it as other than a fabrication. This fits in with the fact that later Christianity was abundantly interwoven with mythological content drawn heavily from **pagan** sources, plus a theology which was produced as the need **arose to** suit the mentality of the times and protect the hold of a **power-hungry** priesthood over the masses.

Then what about the belief that man is saved from **eternal** damnation by accepting Jusus as his Savior? The notion of **Original** Sin is one which Islam emphatically denies, affirming that every human being comes into the world innocent and sinless. Accordingly, he will be held accountable only for what he himself inscribes upon the unblemished *tabula rasa* of his nature, not for what his ancestor Adam[7] (or anyone else whomsoever) did or did not do. For each human individual is responsible only for his own actions; neither sin nor righteousness are "hereditary" characteriztics which can be transferred from one person to another or which are carried in the "blood" or "nature" of human beings. The Qur'an emphasizes this again and again:

> "No soul earns (anything) but against itself, and no bearer of burdens shall bear the burden of another."
> (6:164)

> "....That no burdened one shall bear another's burden, and that man will have only that for which he makes an effort, and that his effort will be seen, and that afterwards he will be repaid for it with fullest repayment, and that verily, to thy Lord's is the goal."   (53:38-42)

> "And fear a Day when no soul will avail another in anything, nor will compensation be accepted from it, nor will intercession profit it, nor will anyone be helped."
> (2:123)

Hence, to attribute to Allah, the Forgiving and Merciful, His laying upon each new-born infant the intolerable burden of a sin committed by his remotest ancestor would appear to be a denial of His unquestionable attributes of justice, mercy, kindness and compassion toward His creatures. And to further claim that the

---

7   It is to be remembered that Islam teaches that the first man. Adam, was also the first prophet to whom Allah gave guidance for himself and his descendants after he disobeyed Allah and turning to Him in repentance for his sin, was forgiven.

taint of this sin is certain to put every human being into Hell for all eternity unless the Deity sacrifices Himself for His creatures whom He is able to, and should if He is indeed Just and Merciful, forgive, is a denial not only of His unfailing justice and good-will toward His creation but also, it would seem, of His wisdom, logic and reasonableness. Islam emphatically proclaims that no one can be saved from Hell by any means except the mercy and grace of Allah, contingent upon his acknowledging Allah as his Lord, surrendering his whole being to Him, and following the guidance which He has revealed. The Loving and Merciful Allah is able to and does forgive sins if repentance is sincere, and every human soul has direct access to its Source and to His forgiveness without any intermediary or intercessor whatever. Consequently there is no need for a Savior, and in any case Allah Most High alone can save.

Another major point of difference between Islam and Christianity is in the doctrine of the Trinity. If Allah is One, as Christians profess to believe just as Muslims do, there is no way by which He can at the same time be Three; even a very young child can grasp the obvious truth of this. The Trinity is usually explained by Christians as meaning not three Allahs but three parts or persons of the One Allah having different functions. But Allah is not like a pie or an apple which can be divided into three thirds which form one whole; if Allah is three persons or possesses three parts, He is assuredly not the Single, Unique, Indivisible Being which Allah is and which Christianity professes to believe in. To Muslims this makes absolutely no sense, and even if it is explained as being a "Mystery" too high for any human mind to grasp, belief in the Trinity is regarded by Islam, as we have seen in the Qur'anic verses just cited, as a form of polytheism. For all these reasons, Muslims hold that they themselves are much closer to the teachings of Jusus (Allah's peace and blessings be on him) than is the Christianity of the Church which, they feel, has tampered with and distorted the Message which the Holy Messenger Jusus brought by ascribing divinity to him.

Such differences in viewpoint, however, should not be taken as grounds for antagonism or heated theological arguments between Muslims and Christians. The Qur'an admonishes:

> "And do not dispute with the People of the Scripture unless it be in (a way) which is better, except with those of them who are wrongdoers; and say, "We believe in that which has been revealed to us and revealed to you, and our Allah and your Allah is one, and unto Him do we submit." (29:46)

For what is common between the followers of the two faiths is many basic beliefs and the vast legacy of moral injunctions and principles of behaviour inspired by belief in the same Allah and the guidance conveyed by Jusus (peace be on him), which should inspire in them friendship, sympathy and appreciation for the other's sincerity, simply "agreeing to disagree" on their differences. In the words of the Qur'an:

> "... Say (O Muhammad): 'I have submitted my will to Allah and (so have) those who follow me.' And say to those who have received the Scripture and to those who do not read, 'Have you submitted?' Then if they submit, truly they are rightly-guided, and if they turn away, then it is thy duty only to convey the Message. And in Allah's sight are all His slaves." (3:20)

Assuredly, in the face of the almost overwhelming array of problems and evils in the world today, the true Believers in Allah have an obligation to put aside their differences and make common cause *as Believers* in the fight against Atheism, disregard for Allah's laws and every kind of wrongdoing. This struggle is a duty for them all, one in which they should support and reinforce each other. As the number of indigenous and immigrant Muslims continues to increase in the Western world, it is hoped that they will make very significant contributions to the societies in which they live, side by side with other like-minded people, by making Islam's point of view known and drawing upon the vast legacy of its teachings to work toward solutions of the many grave problems and dilemmas confronting mankind.

CONCLUSION

What we have presented here has been a very brief glimpse, a small window, as it were, looking into an exceedingly vast and complex subject. Indeed, the body of Islamic knowledge and exposition, concerned with every facet of beliefs, worship, values, morals and behaviour, both individual and collective, is so immense that scholars have spent entire lifetimes to master some part of this knowledge without being able to contain it all.

But what we have been talking about all through this book, and what that vast reservoir of Islamic knowledge is all about, can readily be summed up in one brief word: submission. The aim and direction of all of it is to help the human individual, in his inward and outward aspects, his physical being as well as mind and soul, his collective as well as his personal concerns, to live a life which is surrendered, by will and by deed, to Allah Most High.

For, human beings, due to their very nature, need, want and in fact *do* submit to something. The only relevant question then is, To whom or what? To be a Muslim is to answer this most fundamental of all the questions facing a human individual by submitting one's life to Allah, the Praised and Exalted, alone, following the guidance of Islam, which consists, in essence, of the instructions of the Lord of the universe to His creatures, all the human individuals of this world both past and present, concerning *how* to submit to Him.

> "Say: 'Verily, my prayer and my worship, my life and my death, are for Allah, the Lord of the worlds. He has no associate. This I am commanded, and I am the first of those who submit.'" (6:162-163)

SOME SUGGESTED BOOKS ABOUT ISLAM

—––––– *The Holy Qur'an* . Translations recommended include those by Marmaduke Pickthall, 'Abdullah Yusuf 'Ali (available in paperback), A.J. Arberry, and Abul 'Ala Maududi (being issued in small individual volumes of which the first eight are now available). Due to the difficulties in translating the sublime language and rhythms of the Qur'an, none of these translations can be considered very adequate, but they are the best available to date. Pickthall's and Arberry's translations are without commentary; Yusuf 'Ali has an extensive commentary but it is not scholarly or very adequate, while Maududui's is an excellent, detailed and very scholarly explanation of the meaning of the Qur'an.

Abul-Ati, Hammudah. *Islam in Focus*. American Trust Publications. Indianapolis, Indiana, 1977. A balanced and comprehensive account of all aspects of Islam by a contemporary Muslim scholar.

Arnold, T.W. *The Preaching of Islam*. Sh. Muhammad Ashraf, Lahore, Pakistan, 1976. An objective and very readable account of the spread of Islam from early times.

Barnabas the Apostle. *The Gospel of Barnabas*. 'Aisha Bawany Wakf, Karachi, Pakistan, 1975. Although the authenticity of this book has not been unquestionably established, it is believed to be an apocryphal account of the life of Jusus which has been lost to the world for centuries due to its suppression as a heretical document. Within it one finds the living Jusus portrayed far more vividly and in character with the mission with which he was entrusted than any of the four New Testament Gospels has been able to portray him. Essential reading for any seeker of the truth.

Bashier, Zakaria. *The Meccan Crucible*. Federation of Students'

Islamic Societies (FOSIS), London, 1978. An excellent and moving account by a modern Sudanese scholar of the Prophet's life and the early part of his mission.

Bucaille, Maurice. *The Bible, Qur'an and Science*. American Trust Publications, Indianapolis, 1977. A translation from the original French, this very interesting volume by a French surgeon compares scientific information and concepts contained in the Bible and the Qur'an. Essential reading.

Mufassir, Sulaiman. *Biblical Studies from a Muslim Perspective*. The Islamic Center, Washington. D.C. An American Muslim scholar analyzes the Old and New Testaments in the light of the Islamic teachings.

Mufassir, Sulaiman. *Jusus in the Qur'an*. Muslim Student's Association of U.S. and Canada, Indiana, 1977. This brief pamphlet deals in an insightful manner with the material presented in the last section of this book.

Nadwi, S. Abdul Hasan 'Ali. *The Islamic Concept of Prophethood*. Academy of Islamic Research and Publications, Lucknow, India, 1976. An in-depth study of the role of the prophethood in human life, and of Prophet Muhammad in particular.

Nadwi, S. Abul Hasan 'Ali. *The Four-Pillars of Islam*. Academy of Islamic Research and Publications, Lucknow, India, 1976. A beautiful and interesting analysis of both the outward and the inner meanings of the Islamic acts of worship by an Indian scholar of world renown.

Nomani, Mohammad Manzoor. *The Meaning and Message of the Traditions*, 3 volumes. Academy of Islamic Research and Publications, Lucknow, India, 1975. A selection of the Prophet's *Hadiths* covering all aspects of faith and life, together with a scholarly commentary.

Siddiqi, Abdul-Hamid. *The Life of Muhammad*. Islamic Publications Limited, Lahore, Pakistan. 1975. An accurate, scholarly biography of the Holy Prophet by a well-known Pakistani scholar.

These and other books about Islam are available from Kazi Publications, 1529 N. Wells Street, Chicago, Illinois 60610 or from Islamic Book Service, P.O. Box 38, Plainfield, Indiana 46168.

GLOOSARY

'abd   Slave, bondsman, servant or creature.

Adhan (or azan)   The Islamic call to prayer, either issued from the minaret of a mosque or among a congregation gathered for *salāt*.

Āhlal-Kitab   The People of the Scripture; those to whom a scripture was revealed by Allah through the prophets, i e , the Jews and Christians.

al-Ameen   The Trustworthy, a title given to Muhammad before his call to prophethood by the people of Makkah in recognition of his upright character.

al-Bait al-Harām   The Sacred House, i.e., the Ka'aba

al-Ghaib   The "hidden" or "unseen" referring to those aspects of Reality which are beyond man's perception, sensory capacities or awareness.

Allah   The Arabic name for Allah.

Allahu Akbar   "Allah is the Most Great," an oft-repeated phrase among Muslims which occupies a prominent place in *salat*.

al-Masjid al-Harām   The Sacred Mosque, i.e., the Great Mosque in Makkah inside which the Ka'aba is located.

Ameer   Leader, commander or head of a community.

'Arafāt   A vast, barren plain near Makkah, the scene of one of the major observances of *hajj*.

ar-Rooh   The Spirit, a title by which the Angel Gabriel is referred to in the Qur'an; *Rooh al-Qudus* and *Rooh ai-*

Ameen (the Holy Spirit and the Trustworthy Spirit, respectively) are additional Qur'anic appellations for Gabriel.

Ashaduan la ilāha illa Allah wa ashaduanna Muhammadan Rasool Allah (or 'abduhu wa Rasooluhu) "I bear witness that there is no deity except Allah and I bear witness that Muhammad is the Messenger of Allah (or His slave and Messenger)," the Islamic *Shahadah* or Declaration of faith.

ash-Shahādah The "witnessed" or "evident." Refers both to (1) the Declaration of faith or creed of Islam and (2) to the visible or known realm of existence which is accessible to man's senses, faculties or awareness.

Assalamu alaikum wa rahmatAllah "Peace be on you and Allah's mercy," a phrase of greeting used by Muslims both in meeting and leave-taking, which is also repeated at the end of every *salat.*

Bismillah ar-Rahman an ar-Raheem "In the name of Allah, the Merciful, the Mercy-Giving," a phrase with which Muslims begin all endeavors or actions, including meals.

Chaddor   The outer garment of the women of Iran, consisting of a long draped cloth covering the head and body.

Deen   Religion or way of life.

Dhul-Hijjah   The twelfth month of the Islamic calender during which the *hajj* and the festival of 'Eid al-Adha take place annually.

'Eid al-Adha   The Festival of Sacrifice occurring at the time of *hajj.*

'Eid al-Fitr   The Festival of Fast-Breaking at the conclusion of Ramadan.

Fard   Obligatory or required.

Fiqh Islamic jurisprudence.

Ghusl A bath with running water.

Hadīth The sayings of the Prophet, often referred to as "the Traditions."

Hajj The pilgrimage to Makkah.

Halāl Permissible.

Harām Prohibited.

Haya Shyness, modesty and careful guarding of propriety.

Hijāb The covering dress of Muslim women which is required by Islam.

Hijrah The migration of Prophet Muhammad from Makkah to Madinah, heralding the foundation of the Islamic society and state.

Hudood Plural of *hadd;* literally, "the limits" imposed by Allah, including the punishments laid down by Islam for various crimes.

Ibadāt Acts of worship such as praying, fasting, *zakat, hajj, dhikr* (the glorification of Allah) and reading the Qur'an.

Iftār Breaking fast at sunset.

Ihram In a general sense, a state in which external involvements are prohibited. Specifically, the state of consecration, as well as the dress pertaining to this state, of the pilgrim during *hajj* and 'umrah.

Ilāh Deity, i.e. anyone or anything who is worshipped, served and obeyed, to whom ultimate allegiance and devotion are given, and to whom sovereignty and absolute authority are ascribed.

Imām Leader.

Imàn   Deep faith and trust in Allah.

Injeel   The Evangel or Good News, the original Scripture revealed to Jusus by Allah.

Islām   Pronounced Iss-Iaam (not Iz-lum). In a general sense, submission to Allah; in the specific sense, the final statement of Allah's guidance to mankind revealed through Prophet Muhammad.

Jihād   Earnest striving or effort, either within oneself, in society or in the world at large, for righteousness and against evil, wrong-doing and oppression.

Ka'aba   The first house for the worship of the One Allah built on earth, situated in Makkah, Arabia.

Khalīfat Rasool Allah Succession to the Messenger of Allah, i.e., the caliphs or heads of the Muslim *ummah* and state after the death of the Prophet. The last of the caliphs was deposed in Ottoman Turkey in 1924.

La ilāha illa Allah, Muhammadu Rasool Allah. "There is no deity except Allah, Muhammad is the Messenger of Allah," the Islamic creed.

Lailat al-Qadr The Night of Power during which the first revelation of the Qur'an came to the Prophet, commemorated annually toward the end of Ramadān.

Madhab   School of Islamic jurisprudence or *Fiqh*.

Mahrem   The "prohibited" degrees of relationship, i.e., those near blood relatives of the opposite sex with whom marriage is prohibited in Islam.

Marwah   One of the two small hills adjacent to the Sacred Mosque in Makkah, the site of *sa'i*, one of the rites of *hajj* or *'umrah*.

Muharram   The first month of the Islamic calendar.

Muhammedan   A name often used, incorrectly, by non-Muslims for the followers of Islam (Muslims). This term has never been used by Muslims themselves and is totally unacceptable to them, as it implies that they worship or that their religion revolves around the man Muhammad.

Mu'min   One who possess *iman* or deep faith and trust in Allah.

Muslim,   Muslim In a general sense, anyone who submits to Allah, including all the true prophets of all times. In the more specific sense, one who submits to Allah by following the religion of Islam. Pronounced Muss-lim, not Muz-lim or Moz-lem.

Muttaqeen   Those who possess *taqwa* or consciousness of Allah.

Nabī   Prophet.

Purdah   A Persian/Urdu word denoting both the covering dress of Muslim women and their not mixing with men outside the family circle.

Qada wa qadar The "measure" of what has been ordained by Allah and His "plan," i.e., the Divine decree.

Qiblah   The direction of Makkah (the Ka'aba) from any point on the globe.

Qur'an   The divinely-revealed Scripture of Islam. Pronounced Qur'an, not Kór-an.

Rak'at   Unit of *salāt*.

Ramadān   The ninth month of the Islamic Calender, the Islamic month of fasting.

Rasool   A messenger of Allah; in the technical sense, a prophet who is entrusted with a divinely-revealed scripture.

Safa   One of the two small hills adjacent to the Sacred Mosque in Makkah, related to the performance of *sa'i*.

Sa'ī   "Hastening between the two hillocks of Safa and Marwah, one of the rites of *hajj* and *'umrah*.

Salāt   The prayers or worship prescribed for Muslims five times daily.

Salāt al-Jum'ah The obligatory Friday congregational worship.

Sawm (or *sīyam*)   Fasting.

Sharī'ah   Literally, "the way"; the code of 'life of Islam, based on the Qur'an and the Prophet's *Sunnah*.

Shawwal   The tenth month of the Islamic calender, during which the festival of 'Eid al-Fitr takes places.

Shī'āh   Those Muslims who adhere to the principle of succession to the leadership of the Muslim *ummah* through the descendants of 'Ali and Fatimah.

Shirk   Associating others with Allah's divinity, either in the form of polytheism or by ascribing authority and sovereignty, or giving one's worship and obedience, to someone or something other than Allah.

Shūra   Mutual consultation.

Sunnah   The practice of the Prophet, consisting of what he himself did, recommended or approved of in others.

Sunnī   Short for *Ahl al-Sunnah wa al-Jama'ah*, the People of the *Sunnah* and the Community, i.e., the majority of Muslims.

Sūrah   Chapter of the Qur'an.

Sūrat al-Fāteha The opening chapter of the Qur'an.

Tahajjud   A non-obligatory *salat* which may be observed during the last one-third of the night.

Taqwa   Consciousness of Allah, comprised of love and fear of Him and the desire to merit His pleasure.

Taraweeh salāt   A special *salat* performed in Ramadan after the
last prayer of the day.

Tawāf   Circumambulation or encircling the Ka'aba while
praising and supplicating Allah, one of the essential rites
of *hajj* and *'umrah*.

Taurāt   The original Scripture revealed to Moses by Allah.

Tayammum   Dry-cleansing preceding *salat* which replaces
cleaning with water *(wudu)* when water is not available
or its use is likely to be injurious to illness.

'Ubūdiyat   The state of enslavement or creatureliness of man
and all the rest of creation in relation to Allah.

Ummah   Community or collectivity.

'Umrah   The Lesser Pilgrimage.

Wudū   Ablution preceding *salat*

Yathrib   An old name for Madinah.

Zaboor   The divinely-revealed Scripture given to Prophet
David.

Zakāt   The obligatory poor-due of Islam.

Zamzam   The well or spring within the compound of the
Sacred Mosque in Makkah.

Index

C

D

E

F

G

L

M

N

O

P

Q

R

S

T

U